DOGS RULE & CATS DO TOO

Created and Illustrated

by Valerie Dowdy

DEDICATED TO ALL DOG AND CAT LOVERS
HAPPY COLORING!

-VALERIE-

ISBN-13: 978-1539724469
ISBN-10: 1539724468

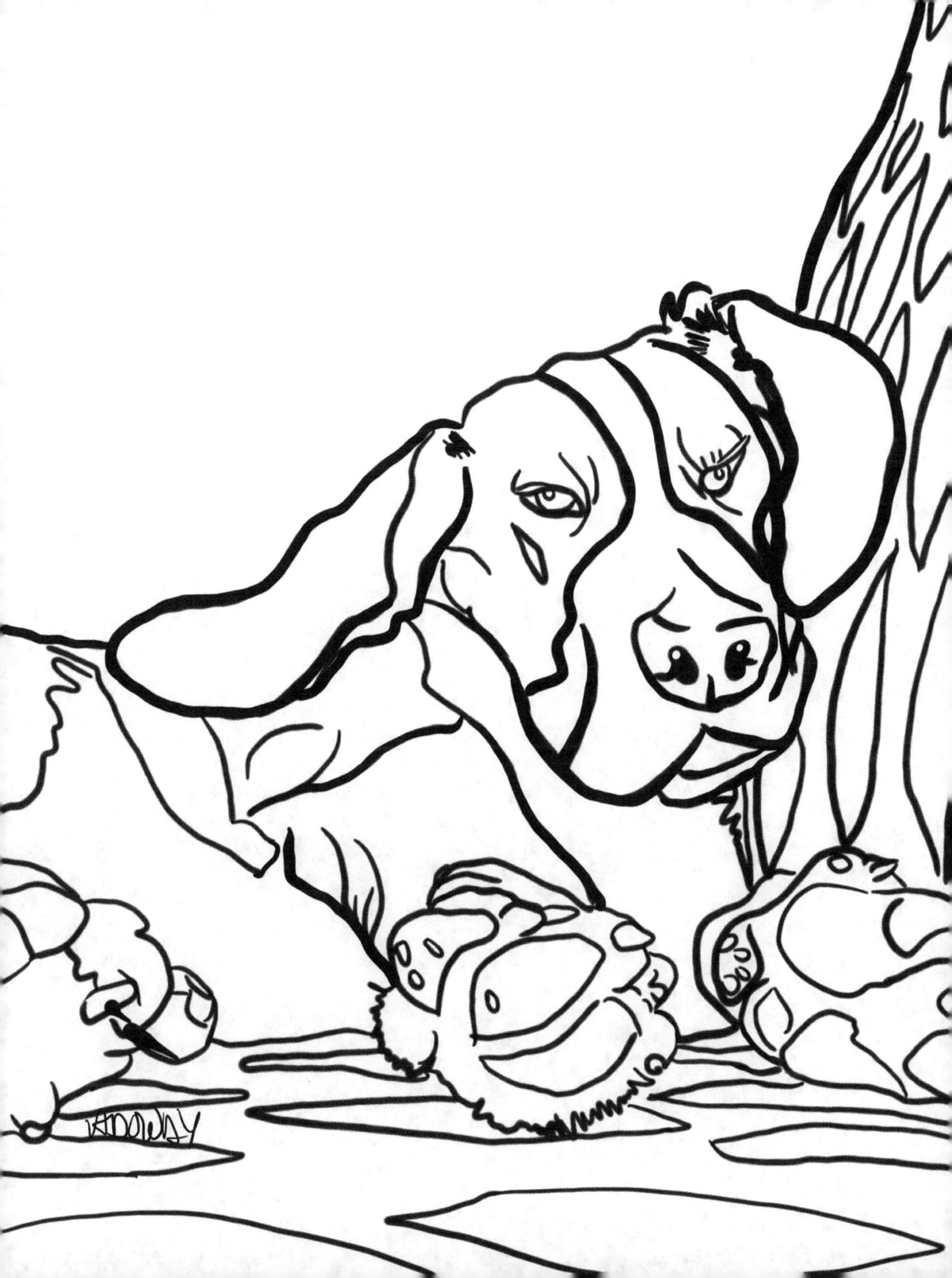

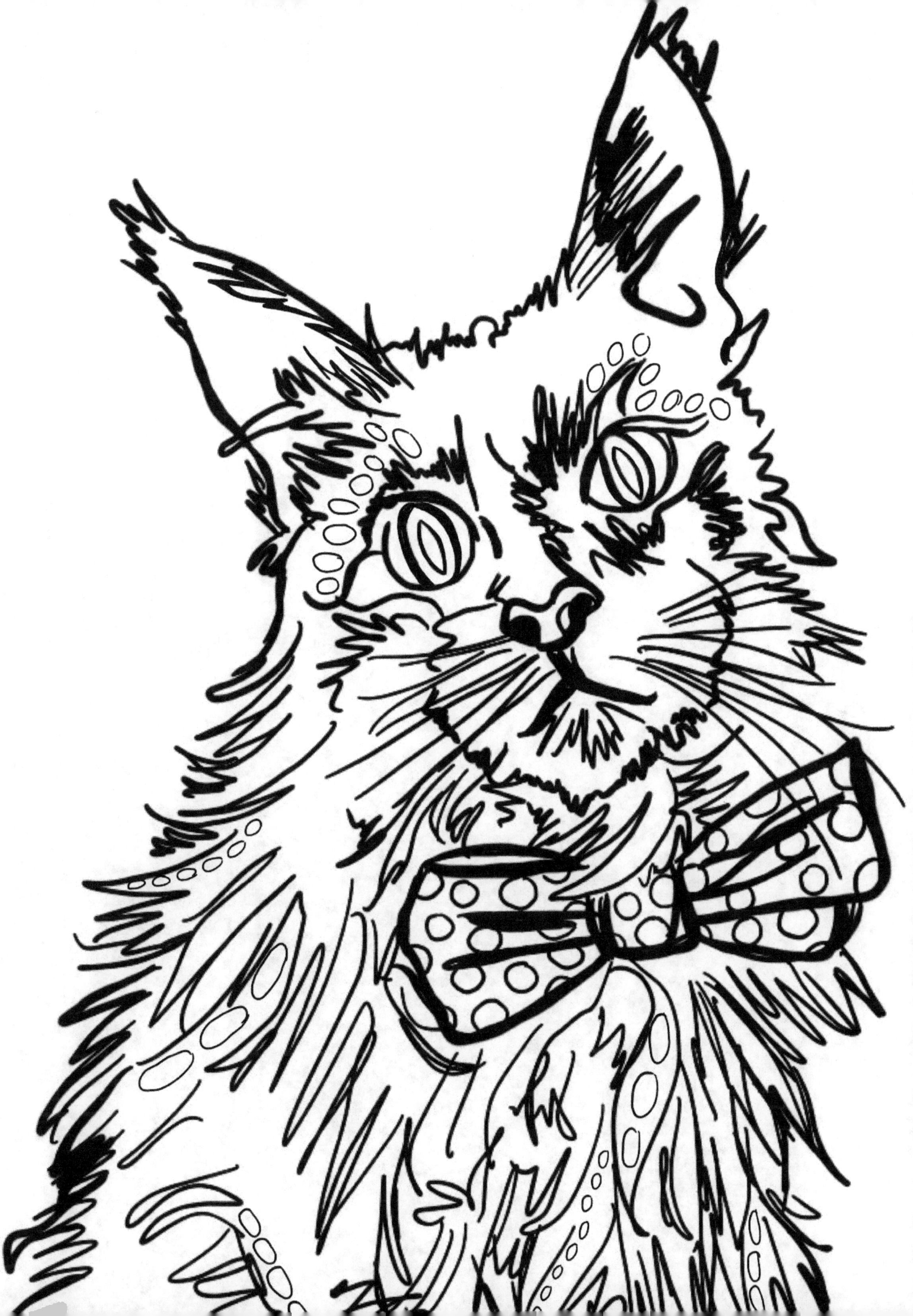

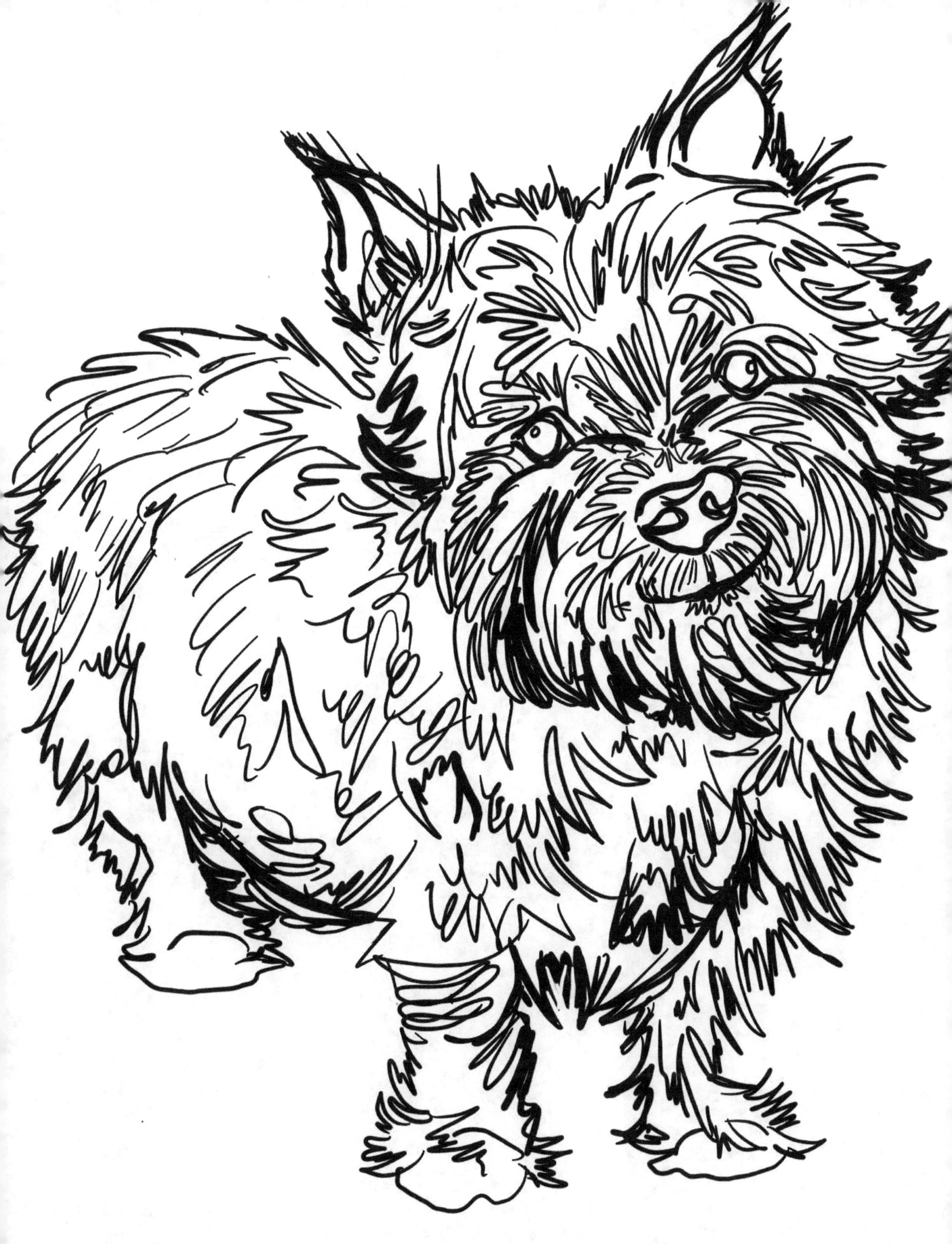

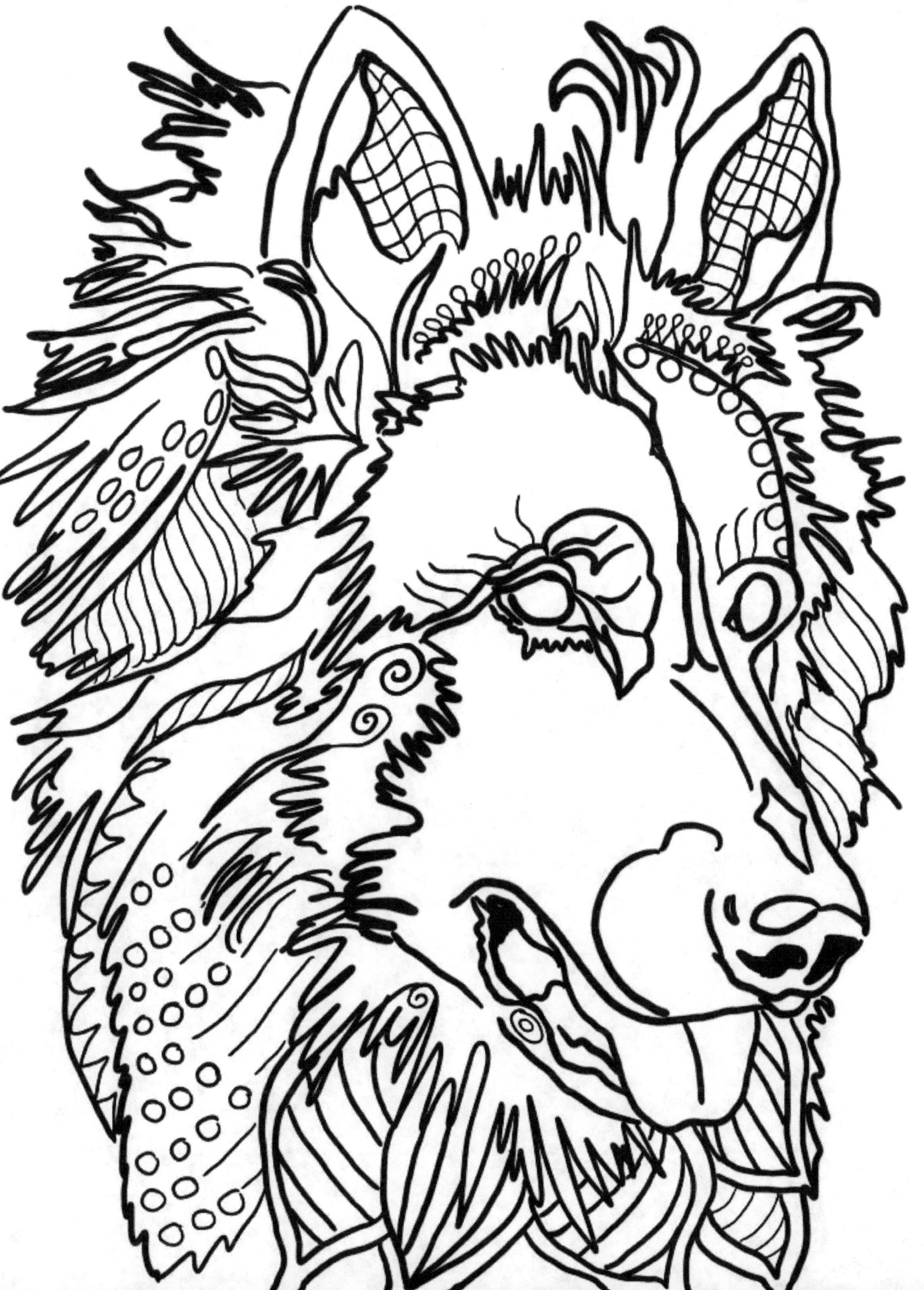

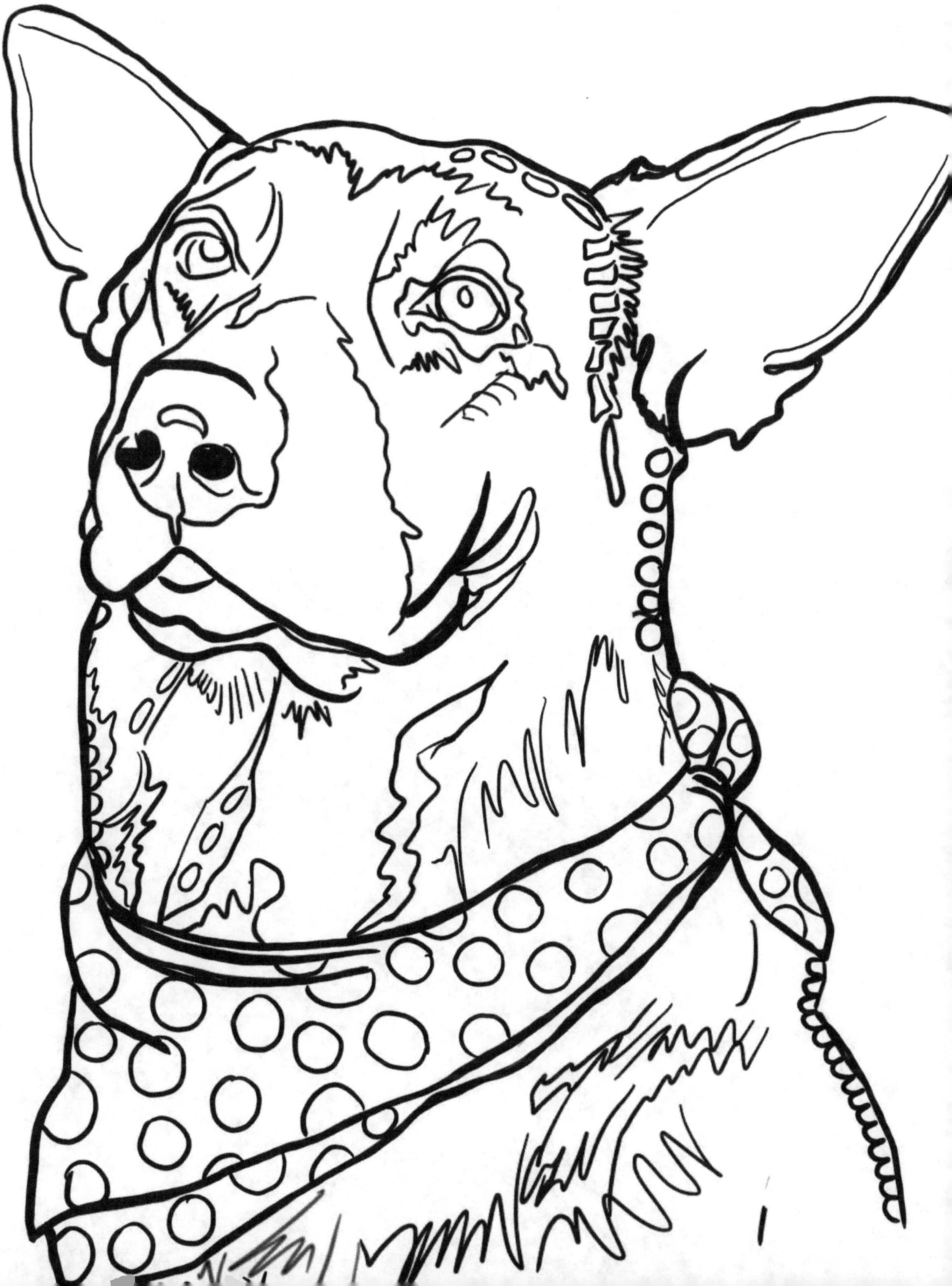

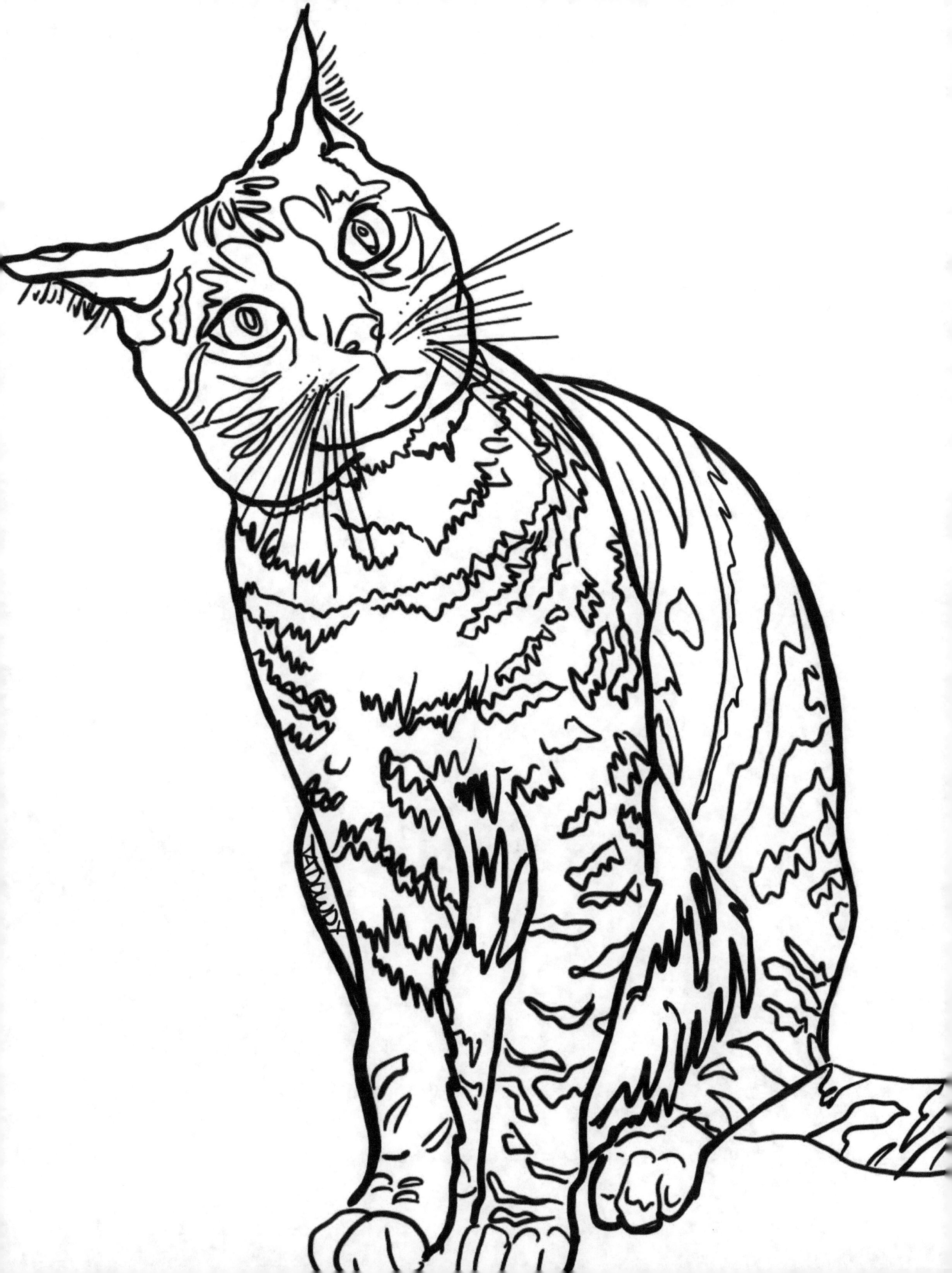

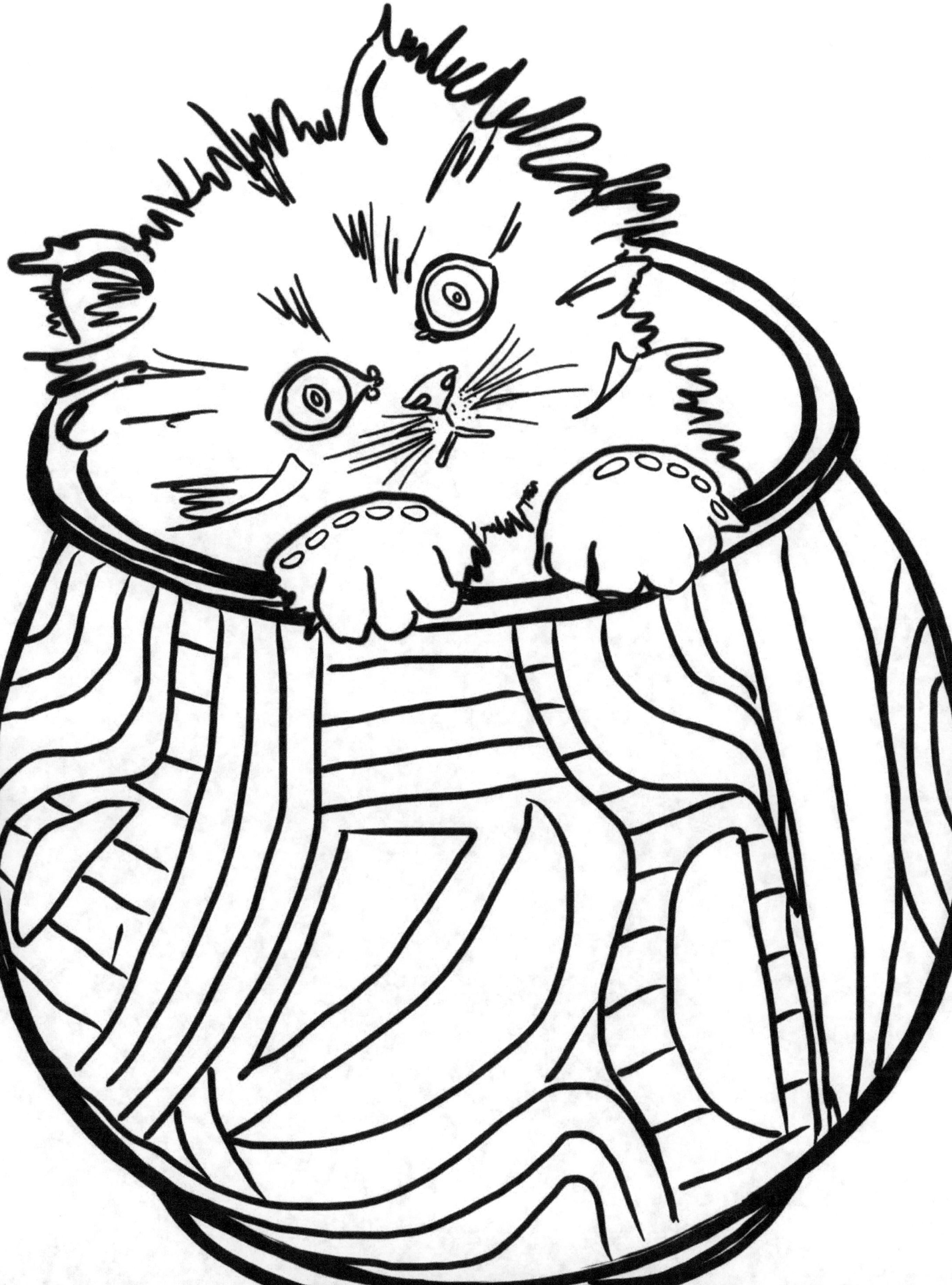

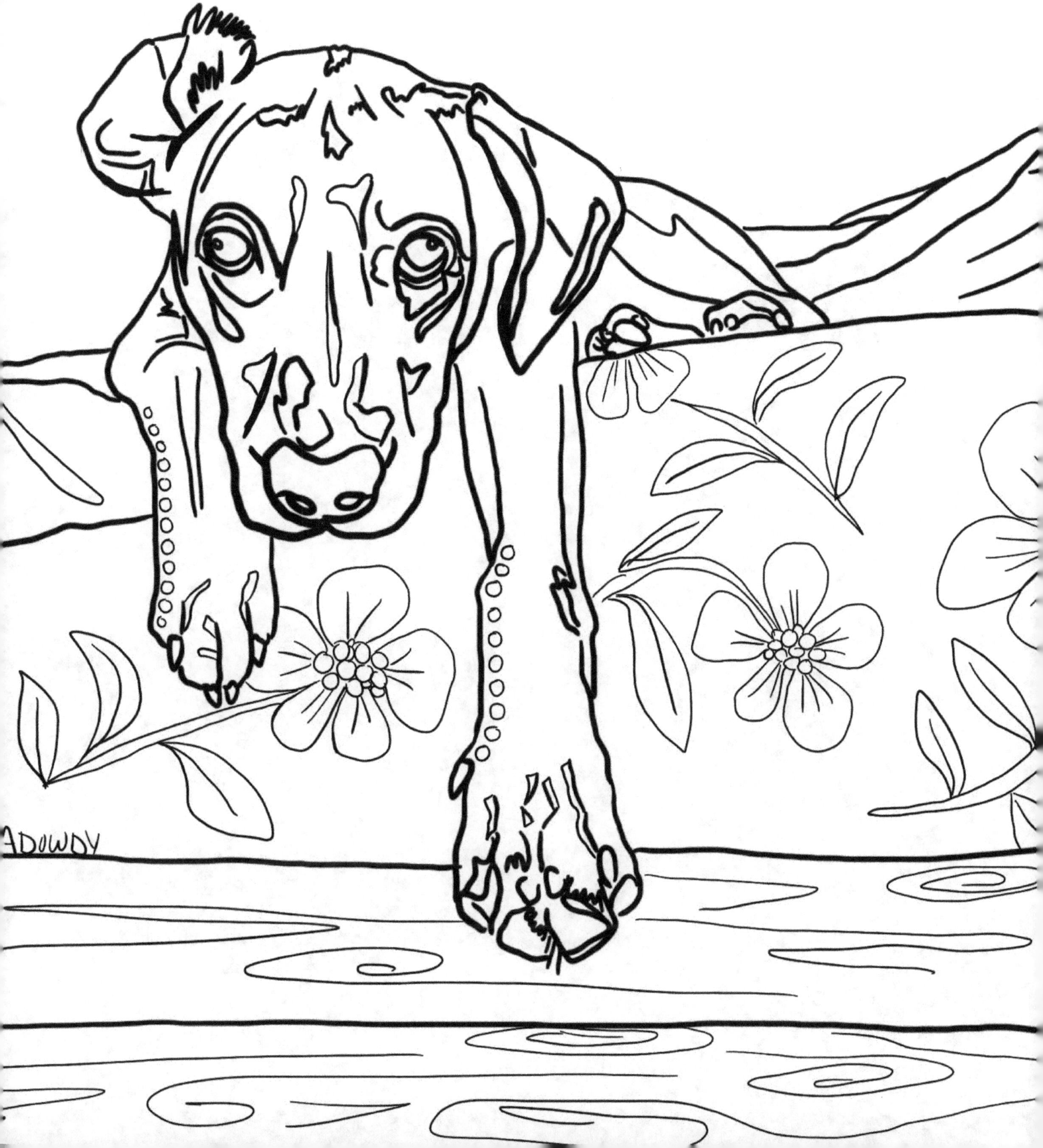
ADOWDY

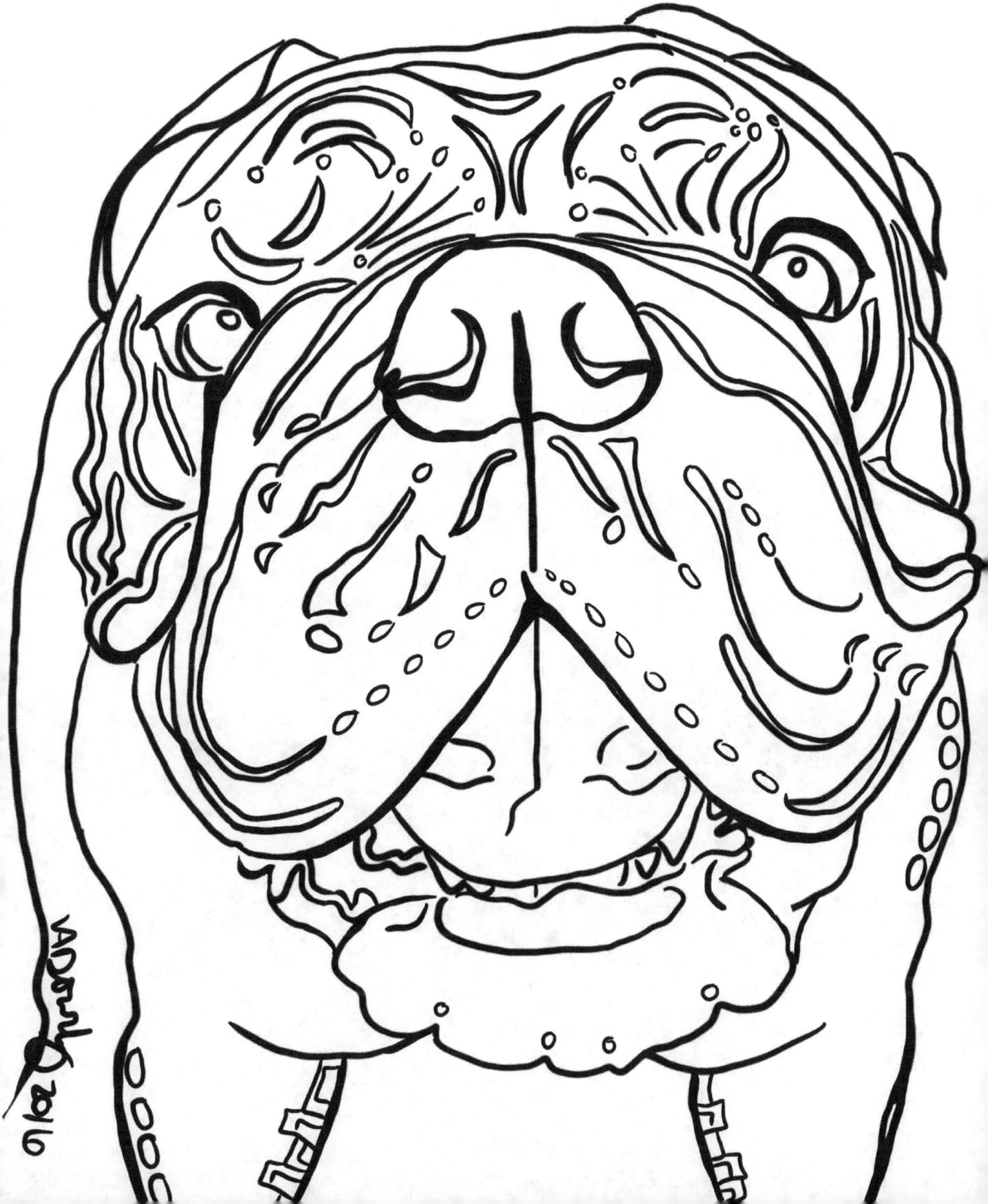

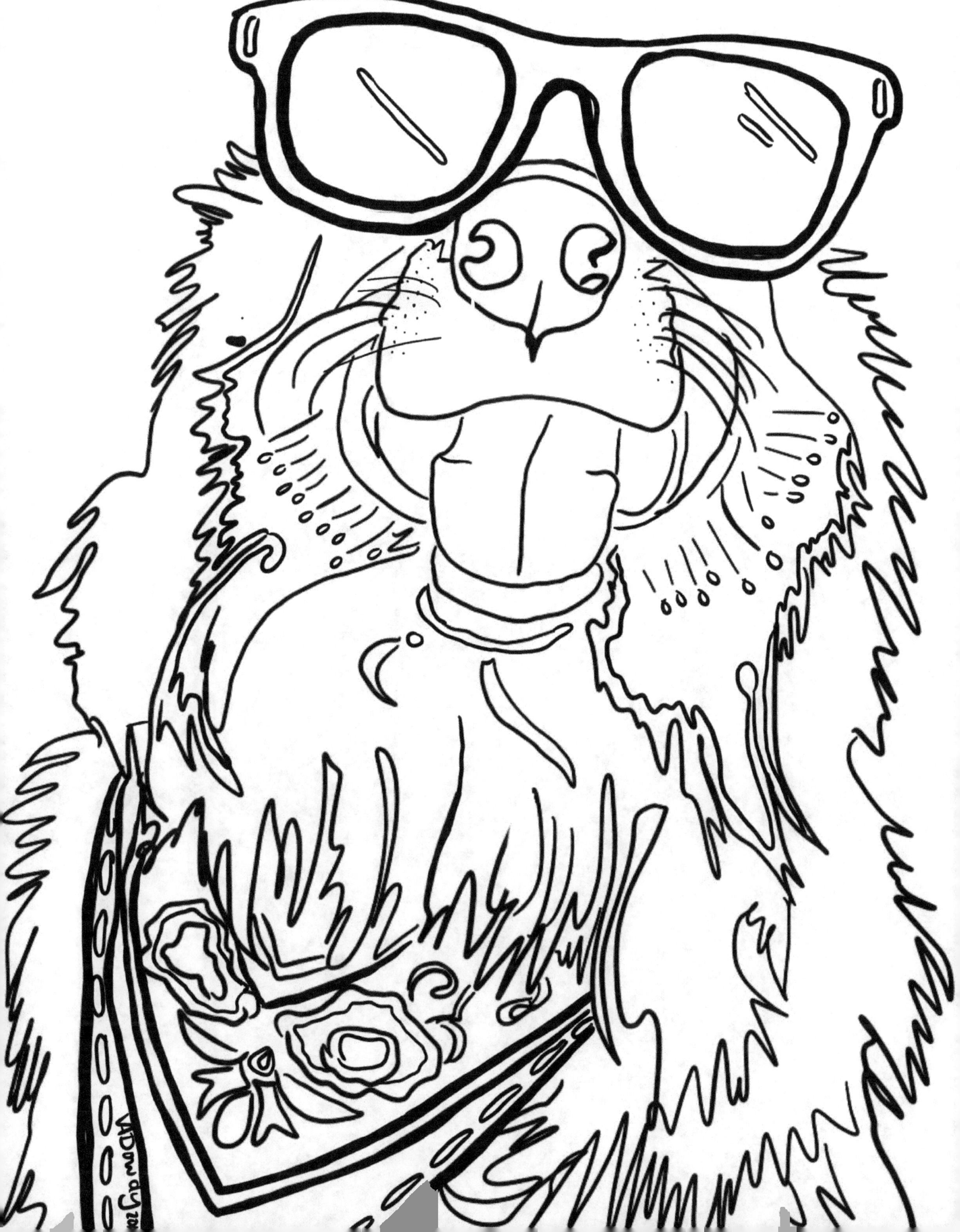

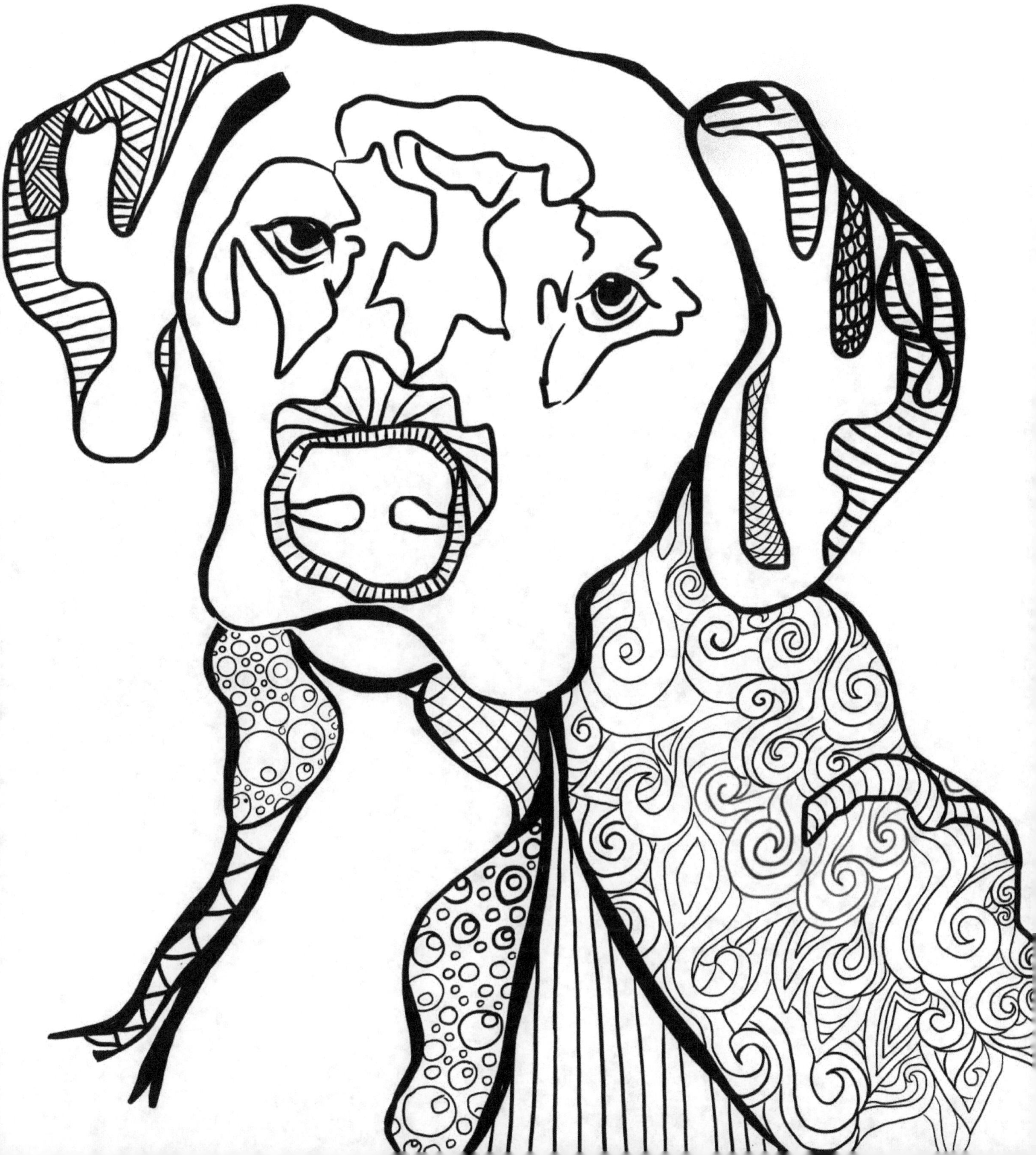

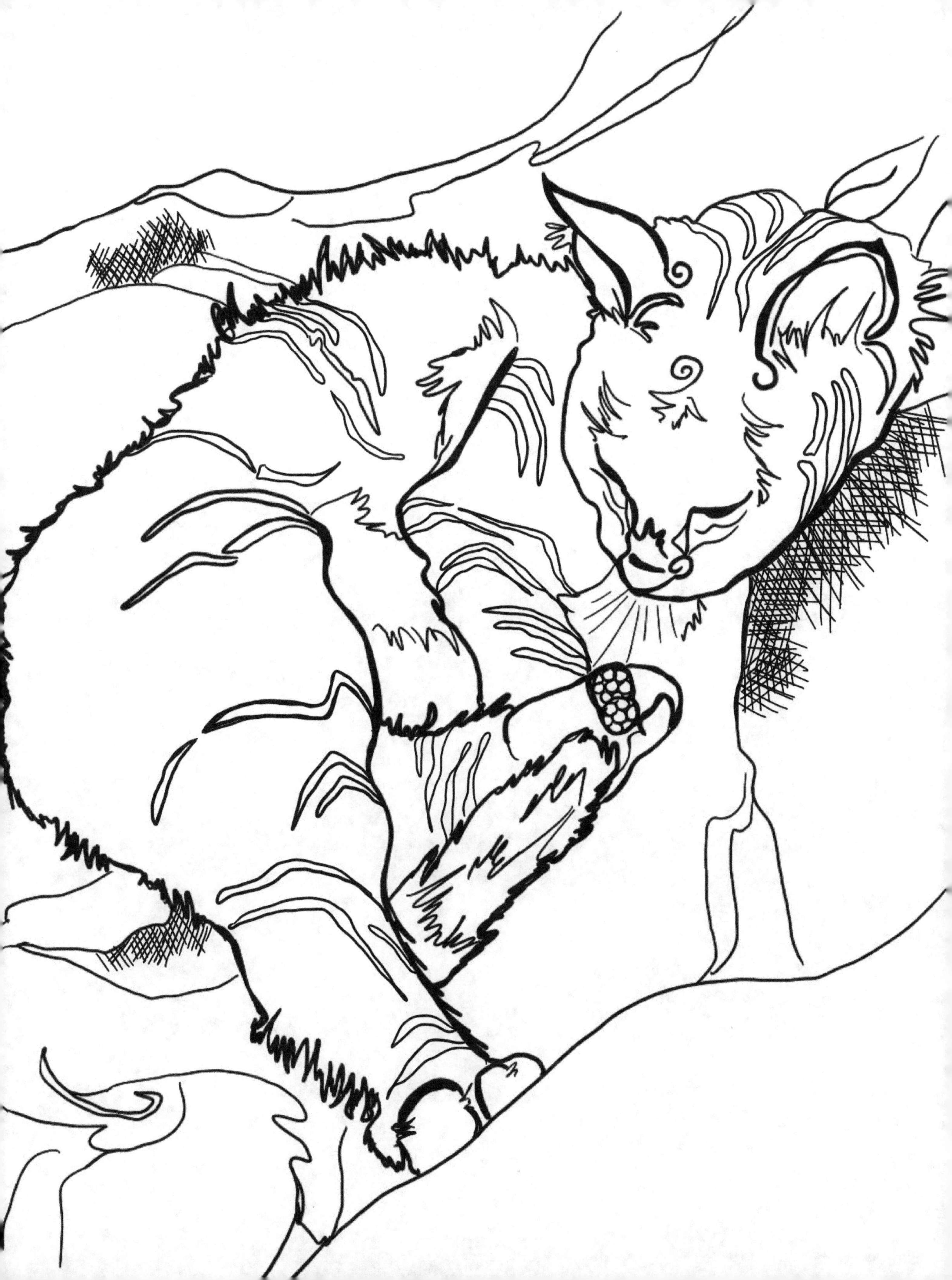

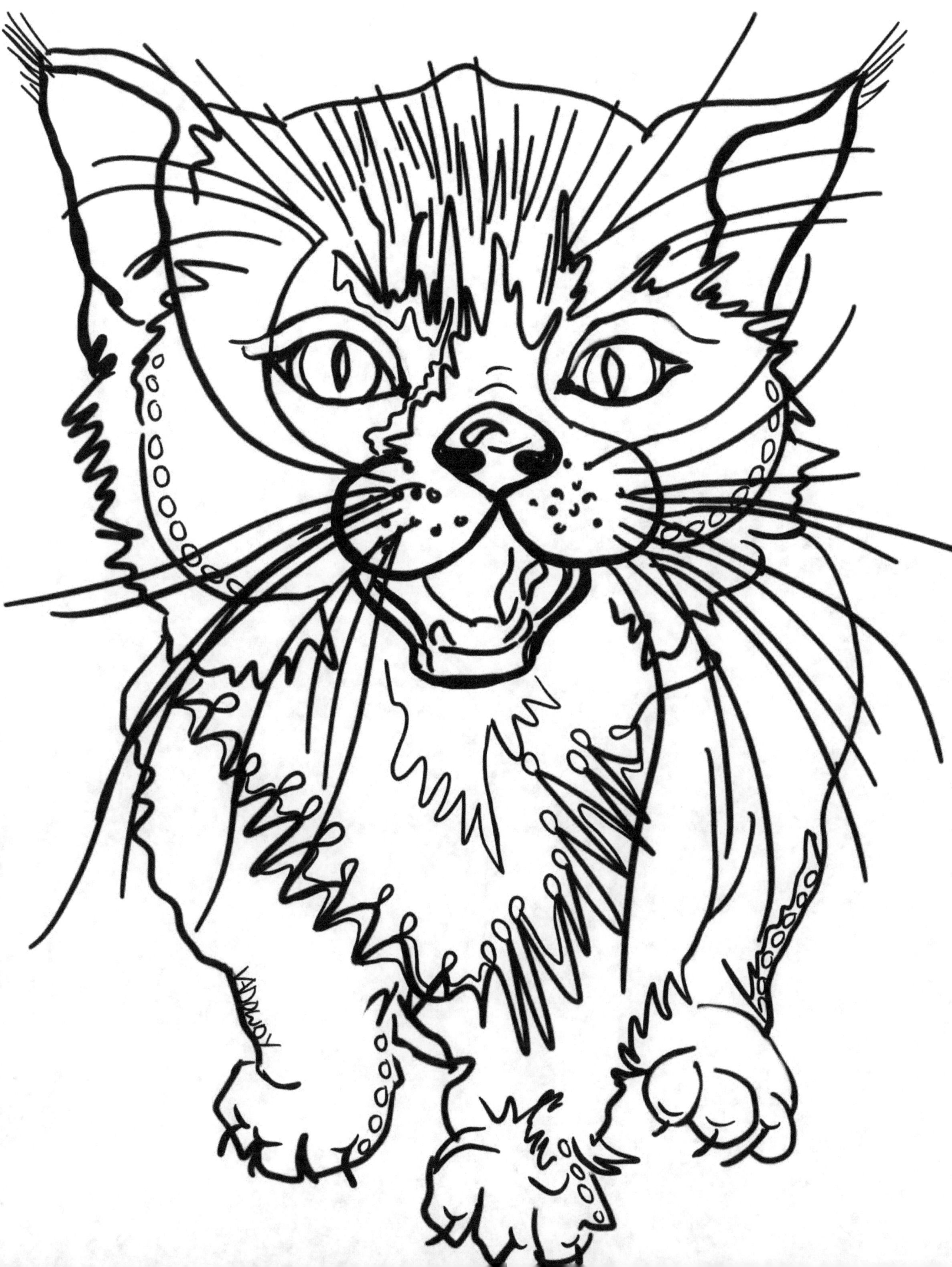

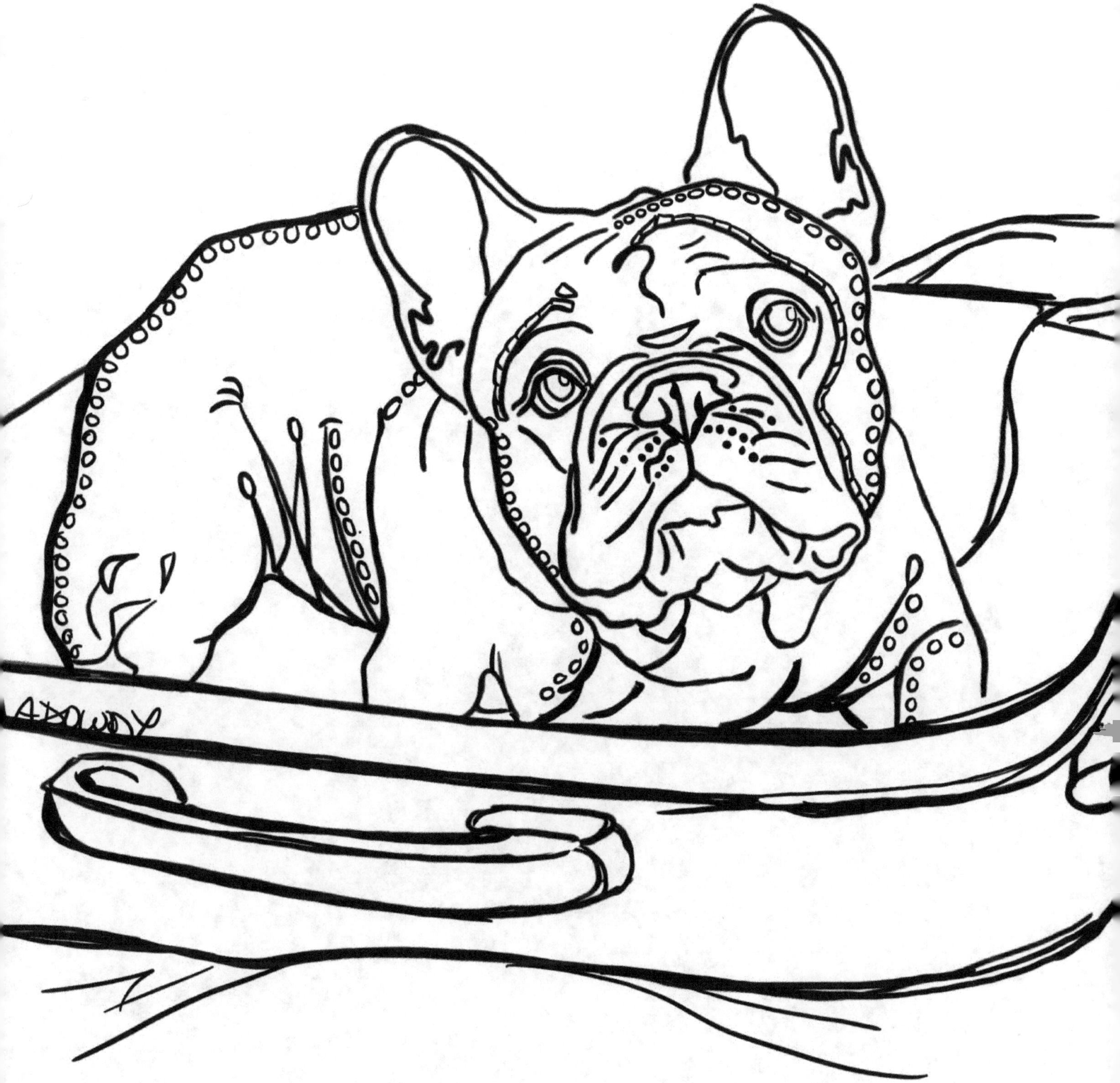

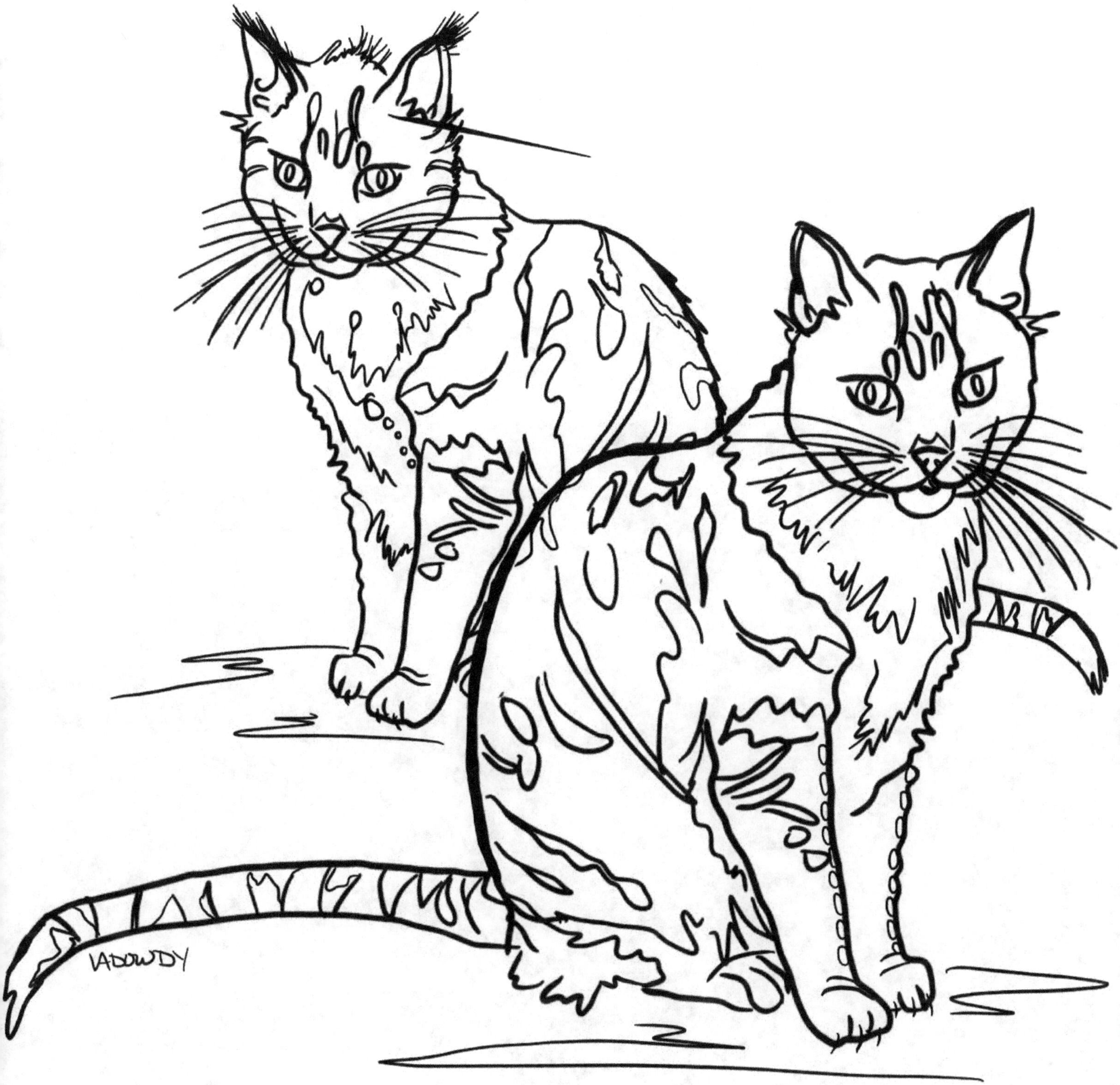
VADOWDY

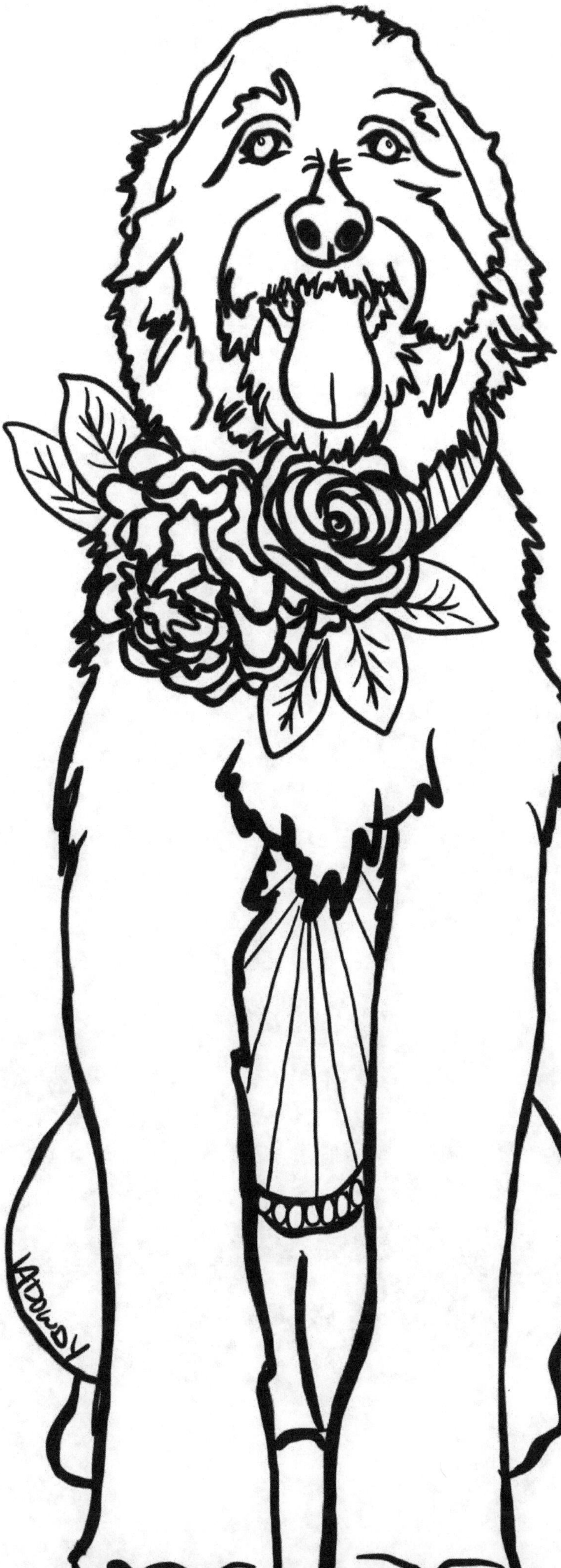
VADOWDY

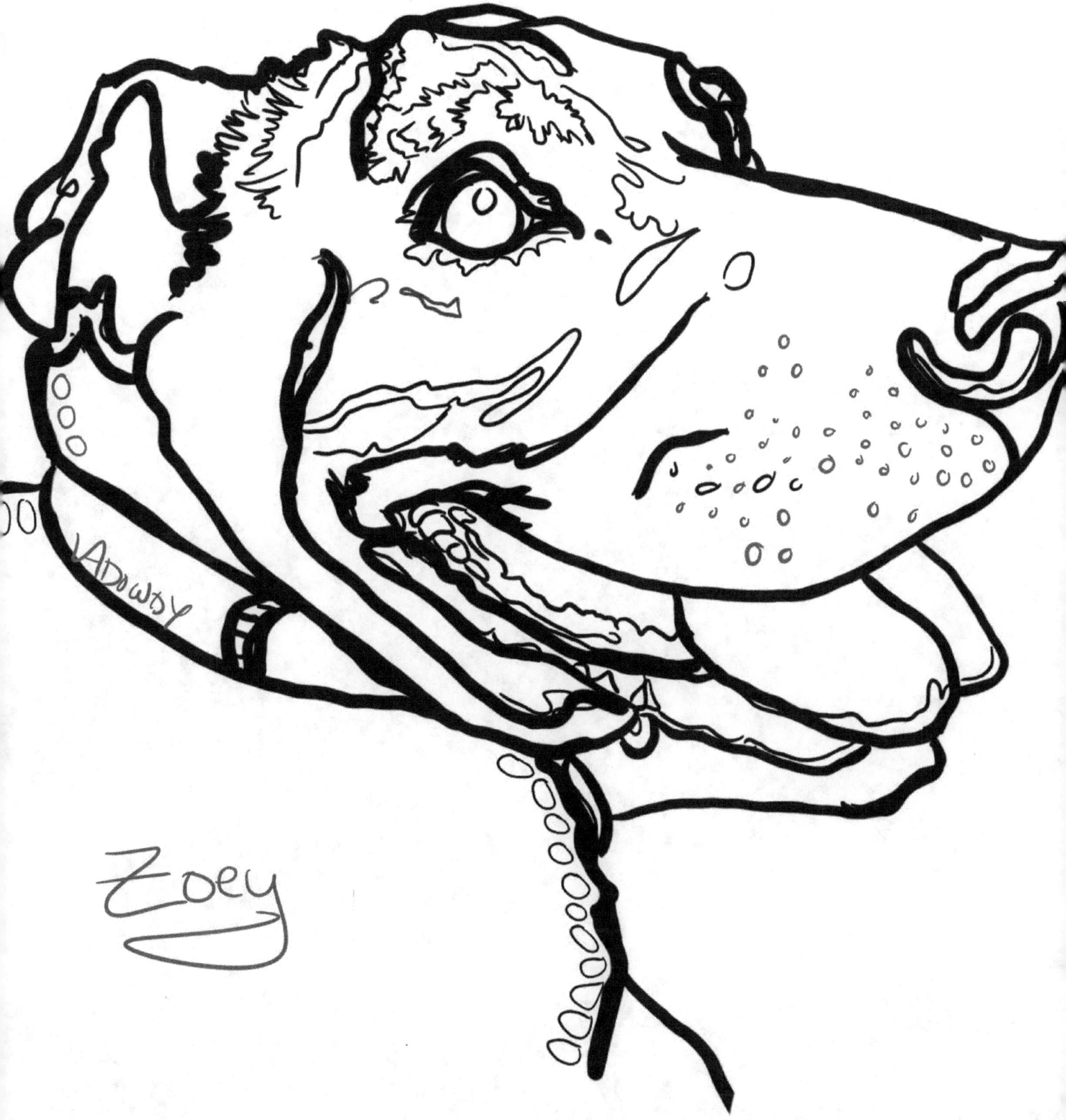
ADOWDY
Zoey

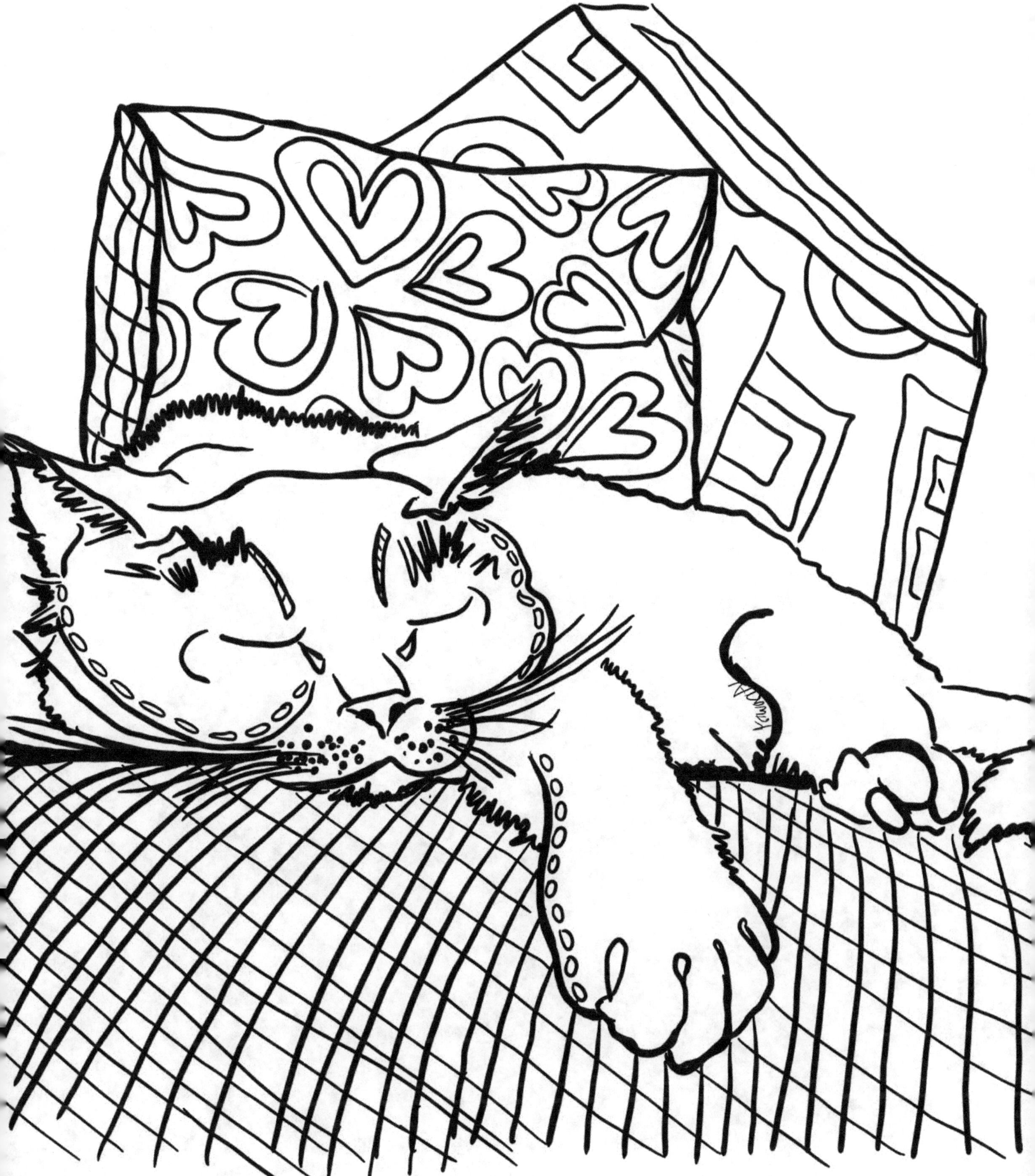

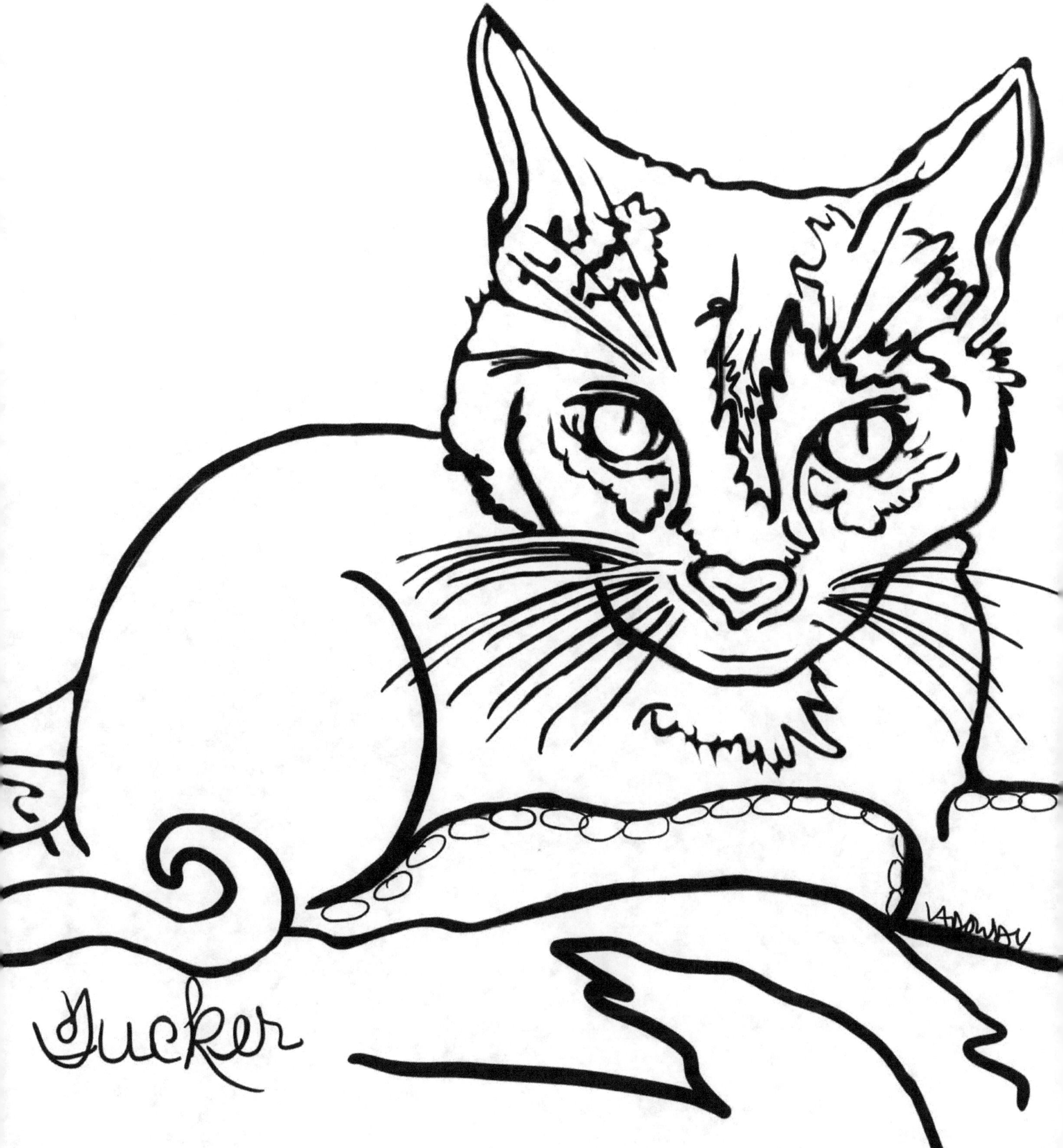
Tucker

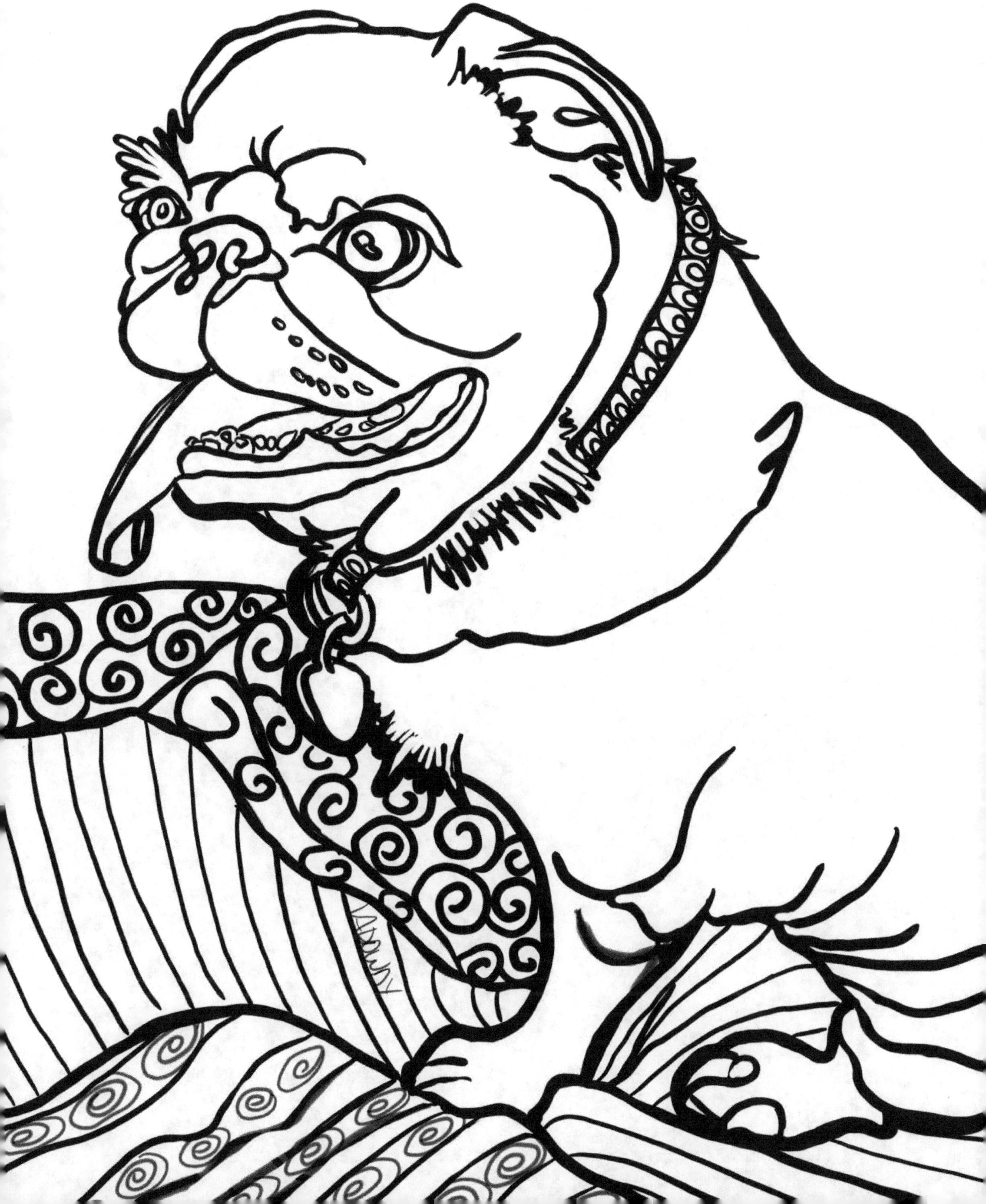

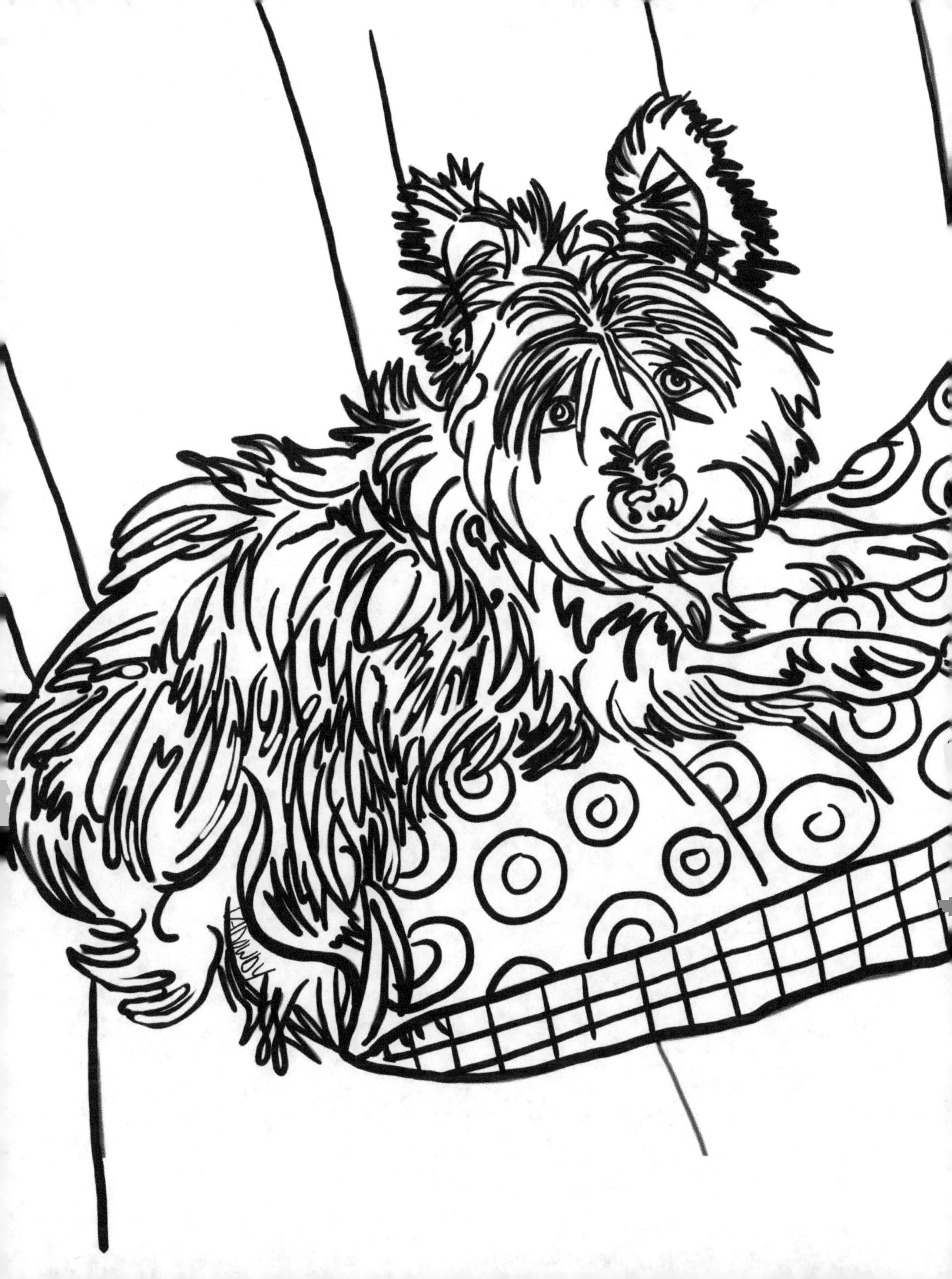

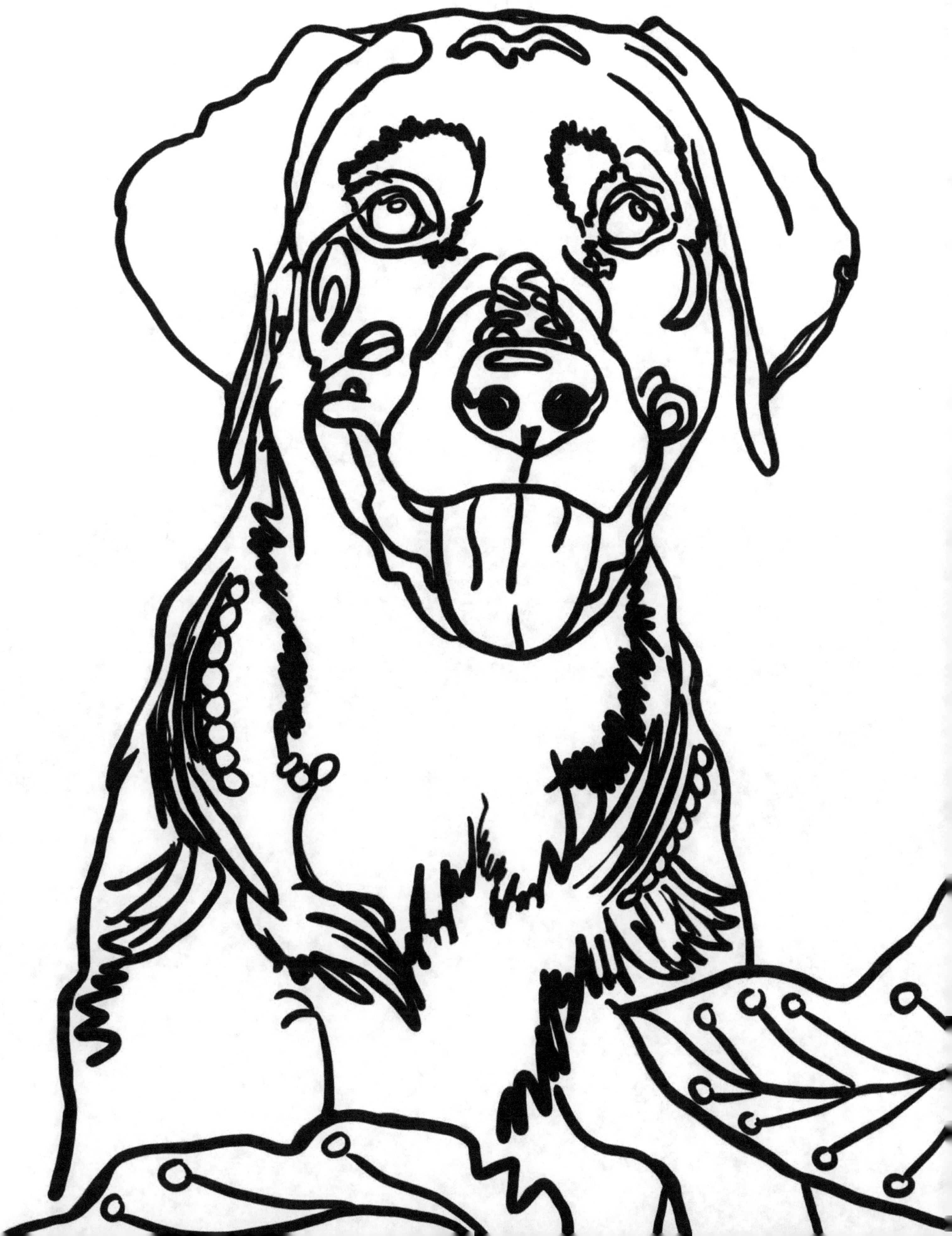

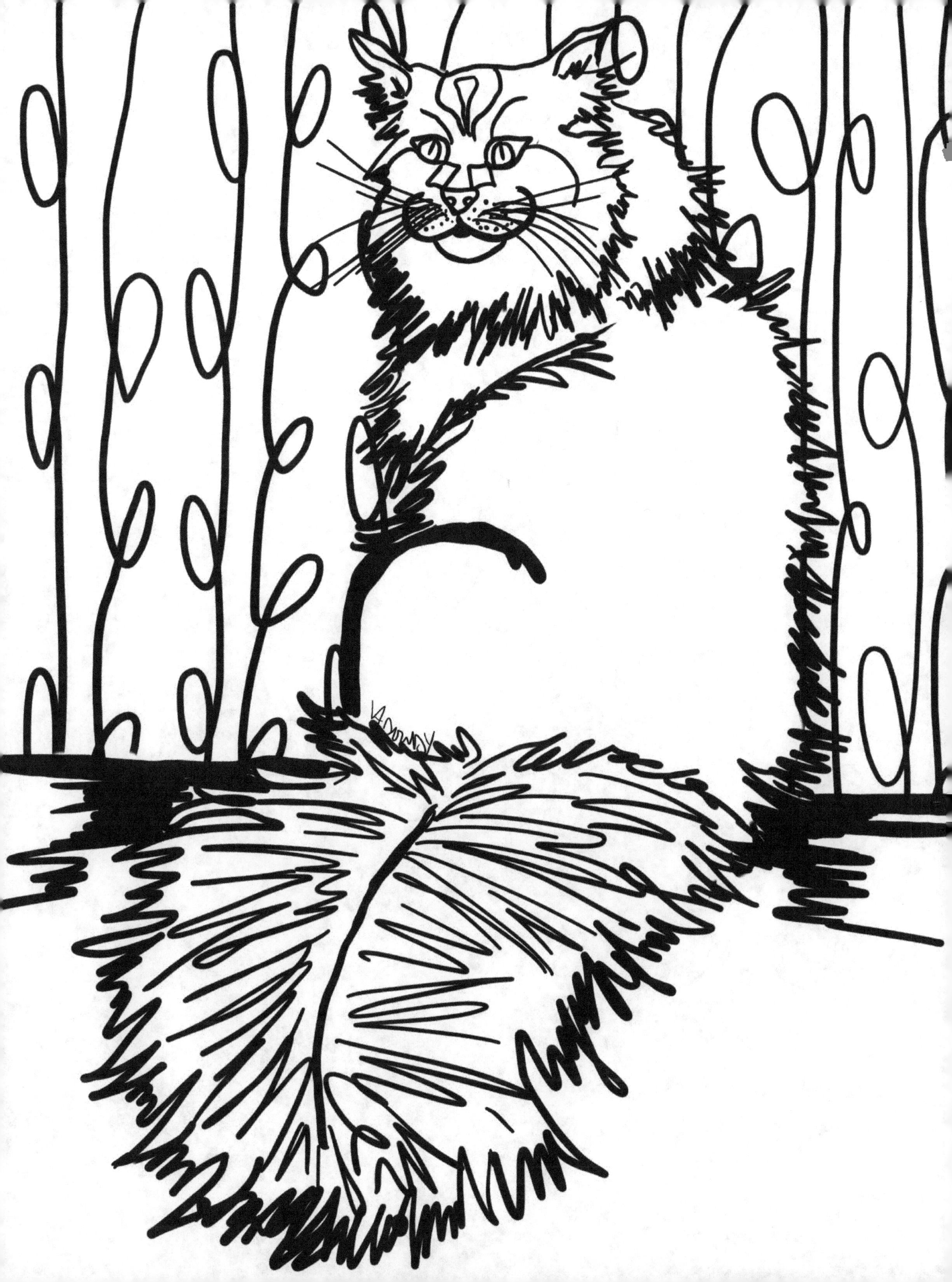

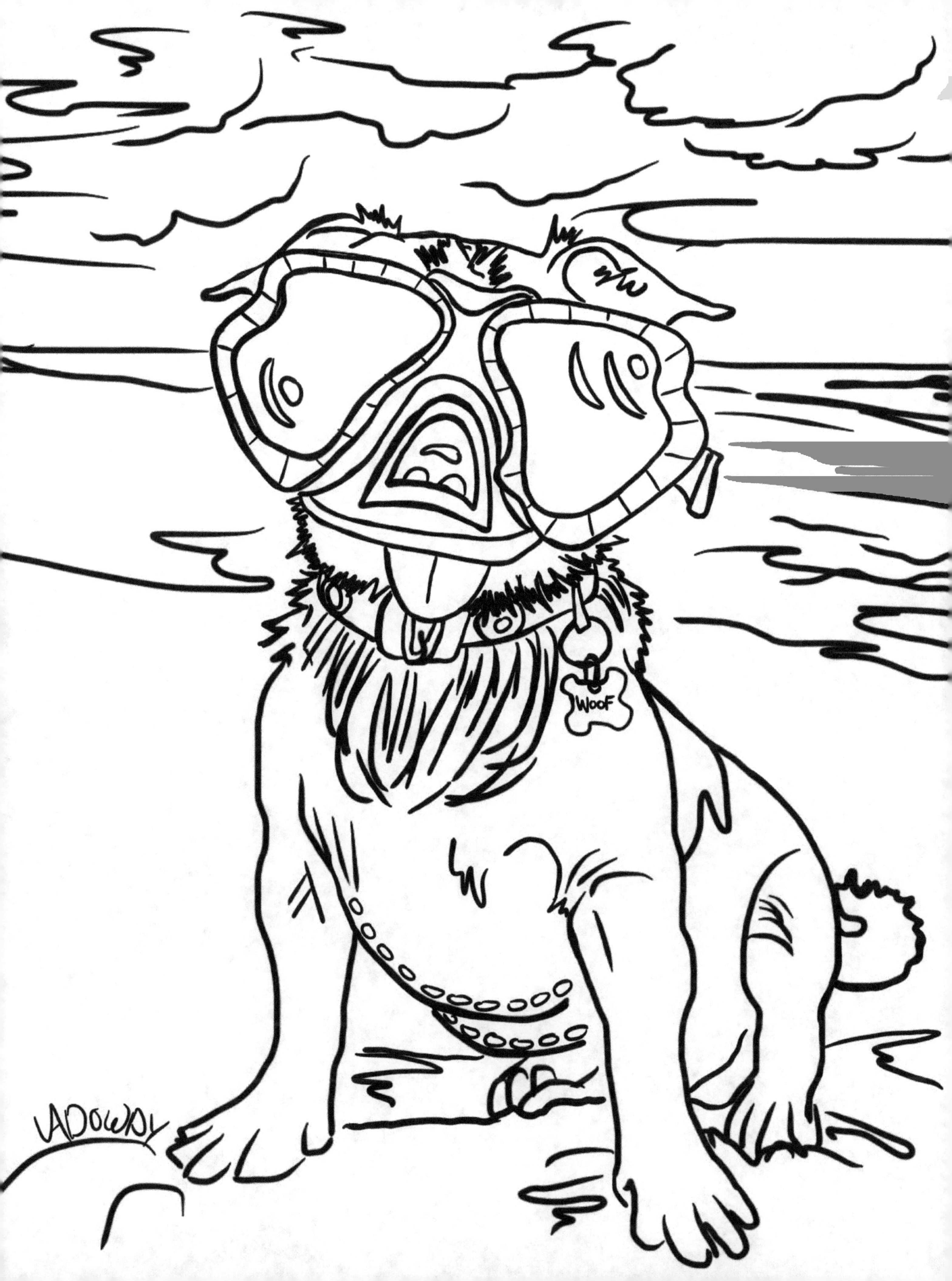
WOOF
VADOWDY

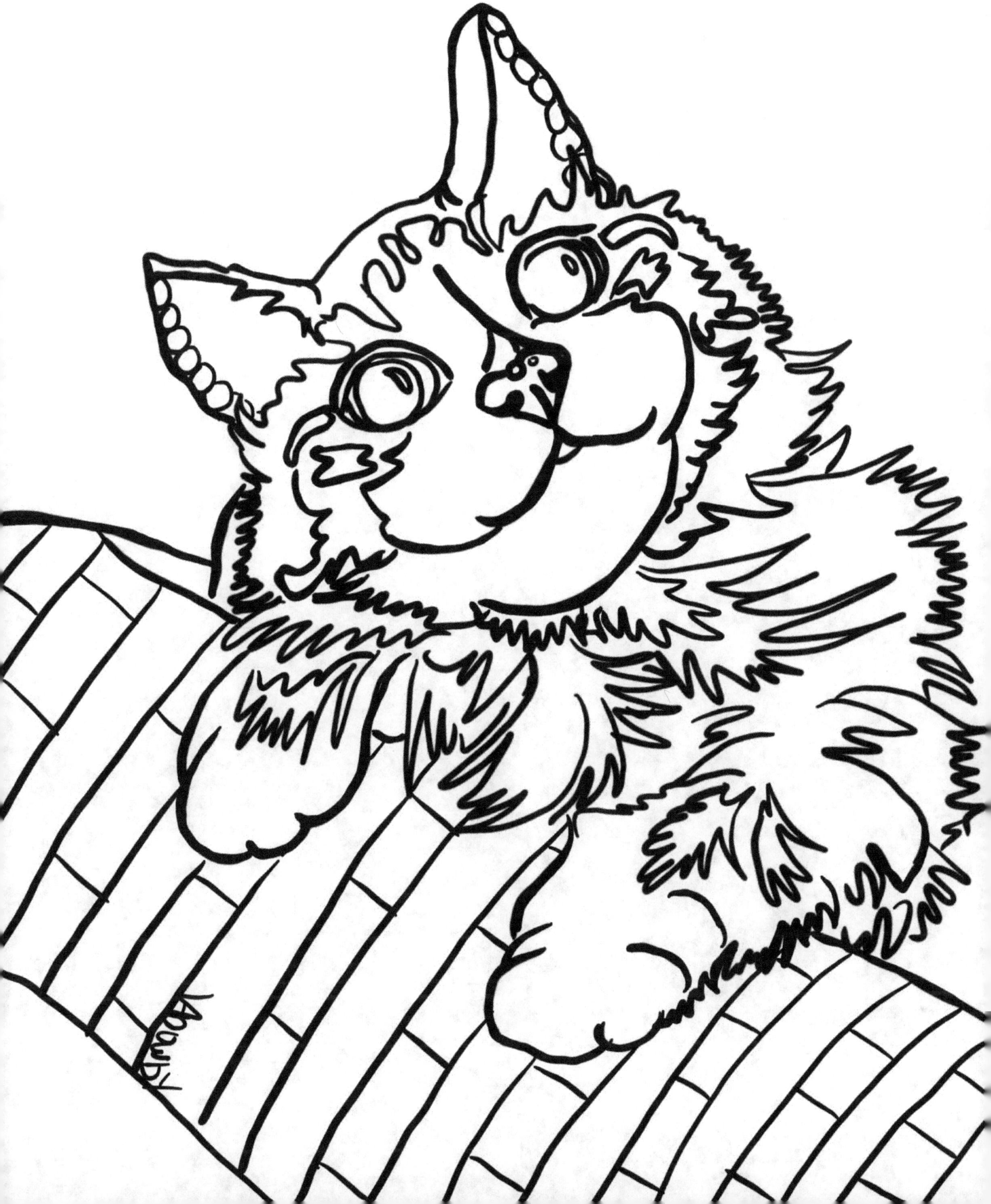

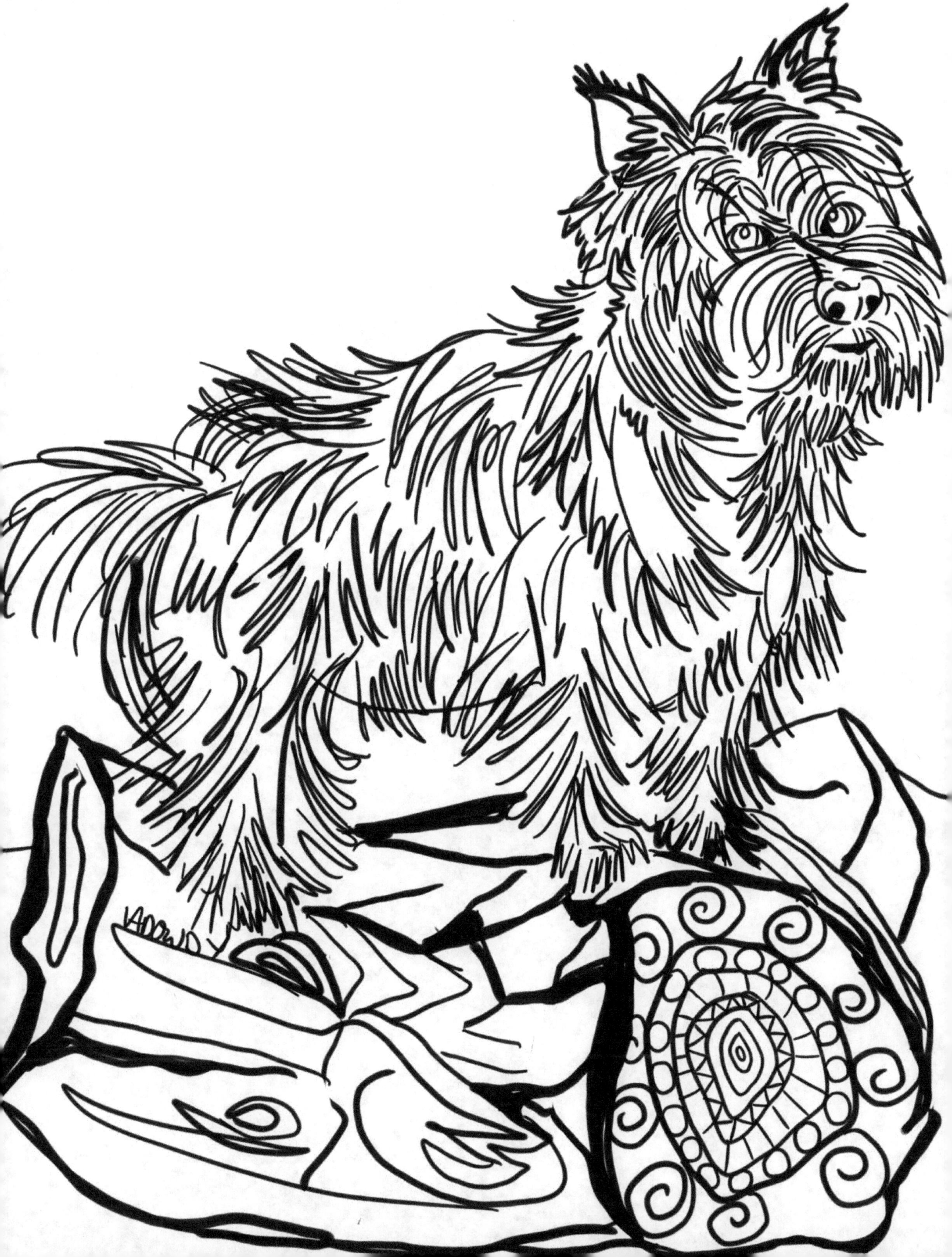

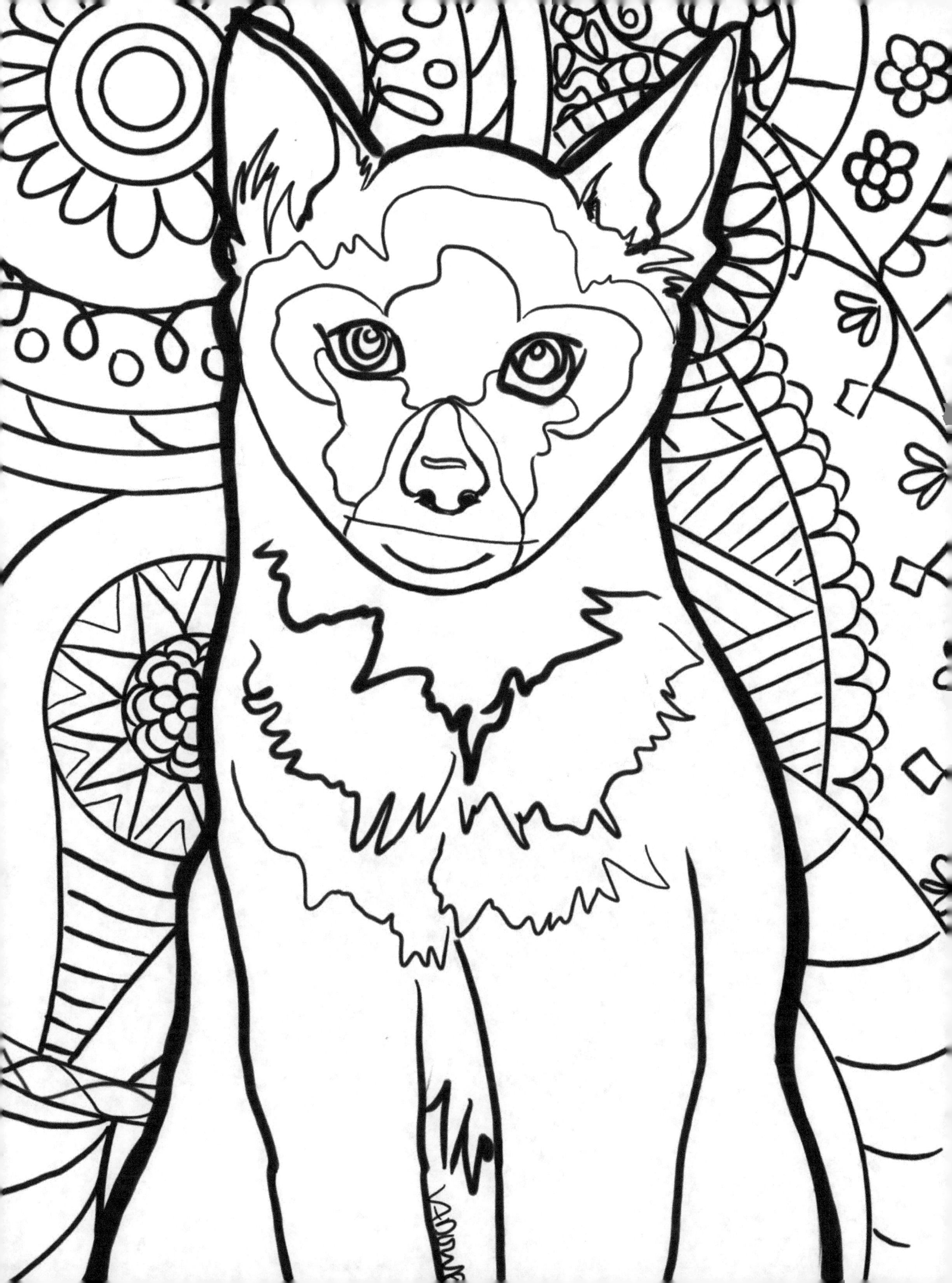

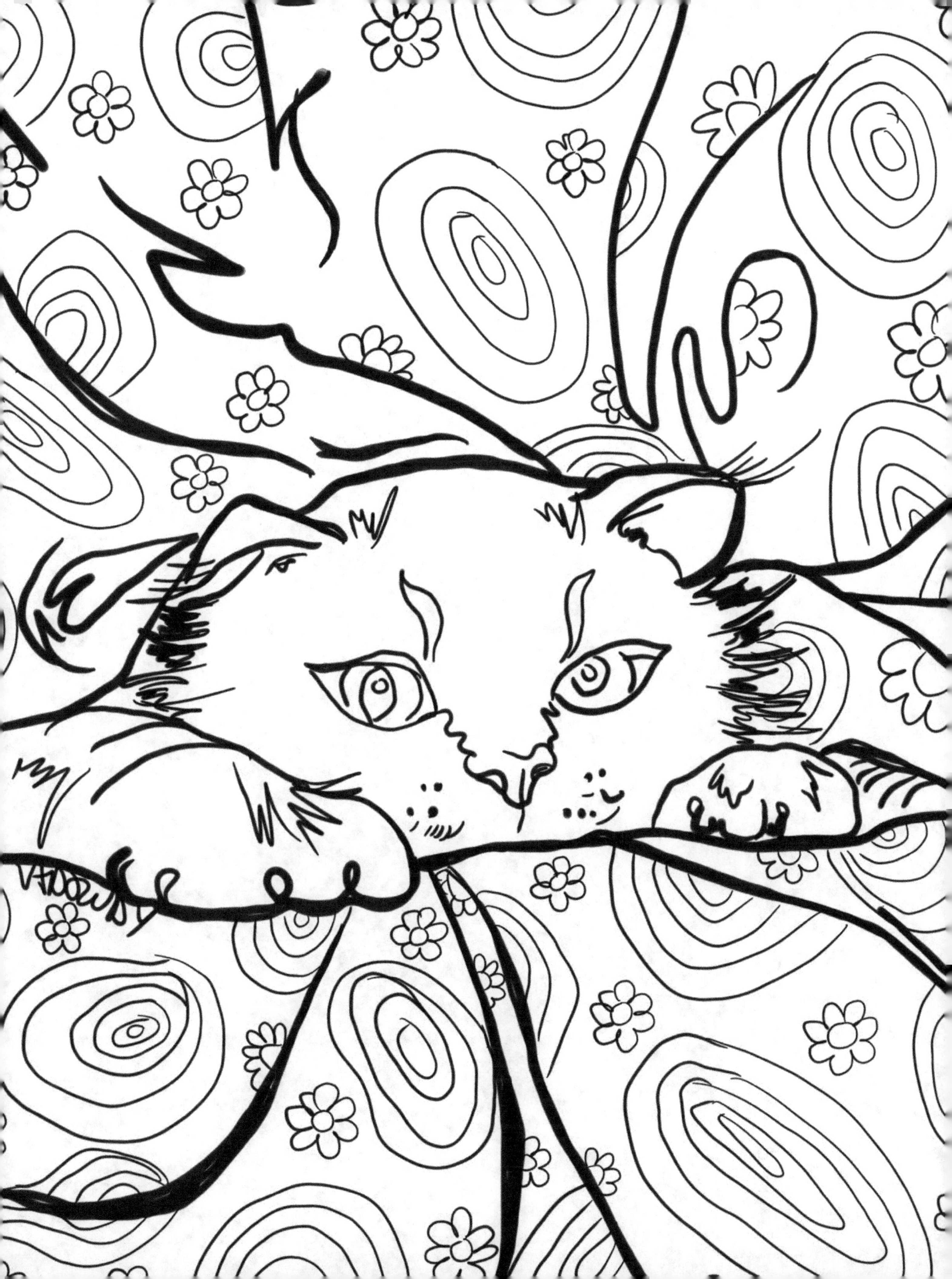

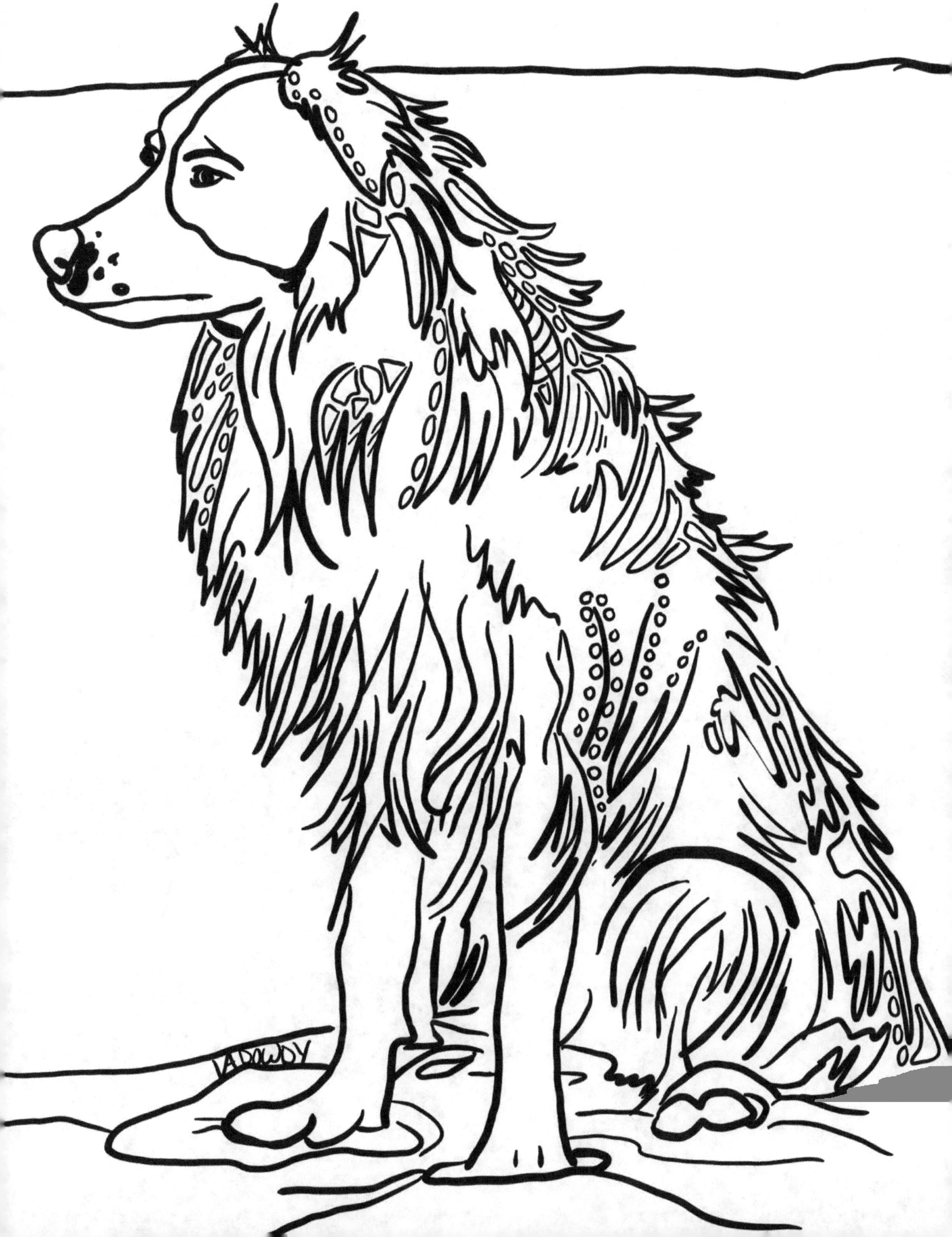
JADOWDY

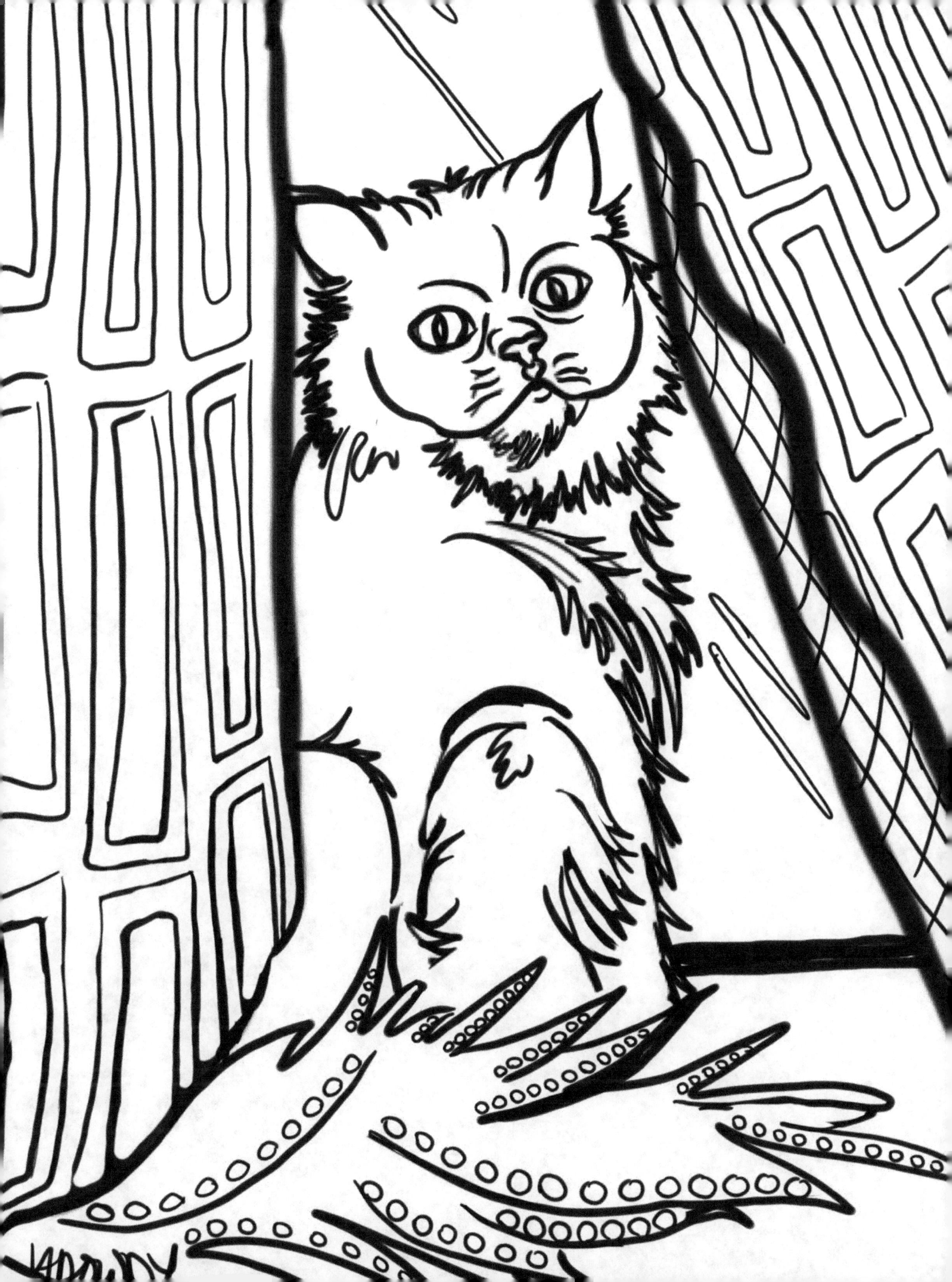

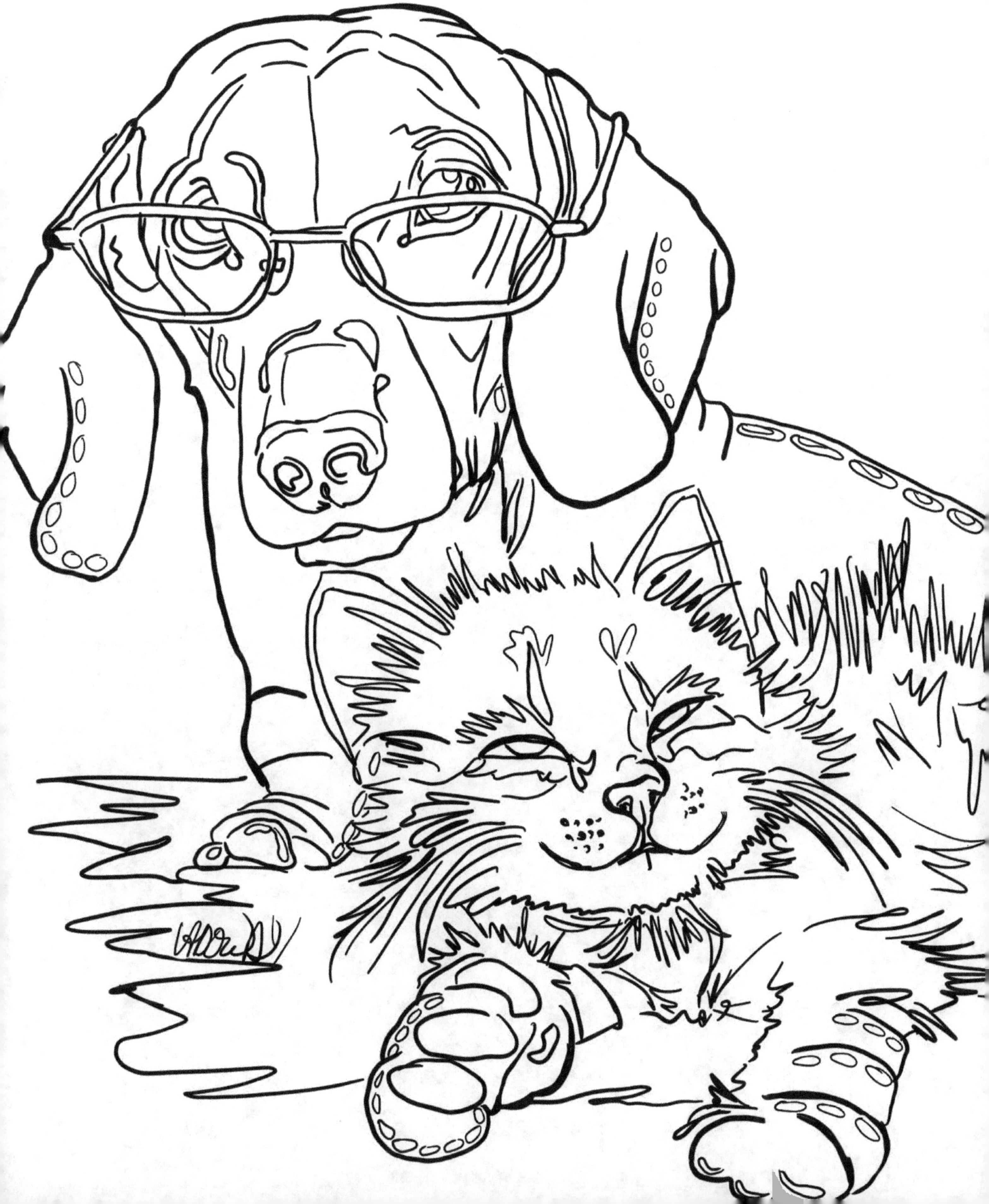

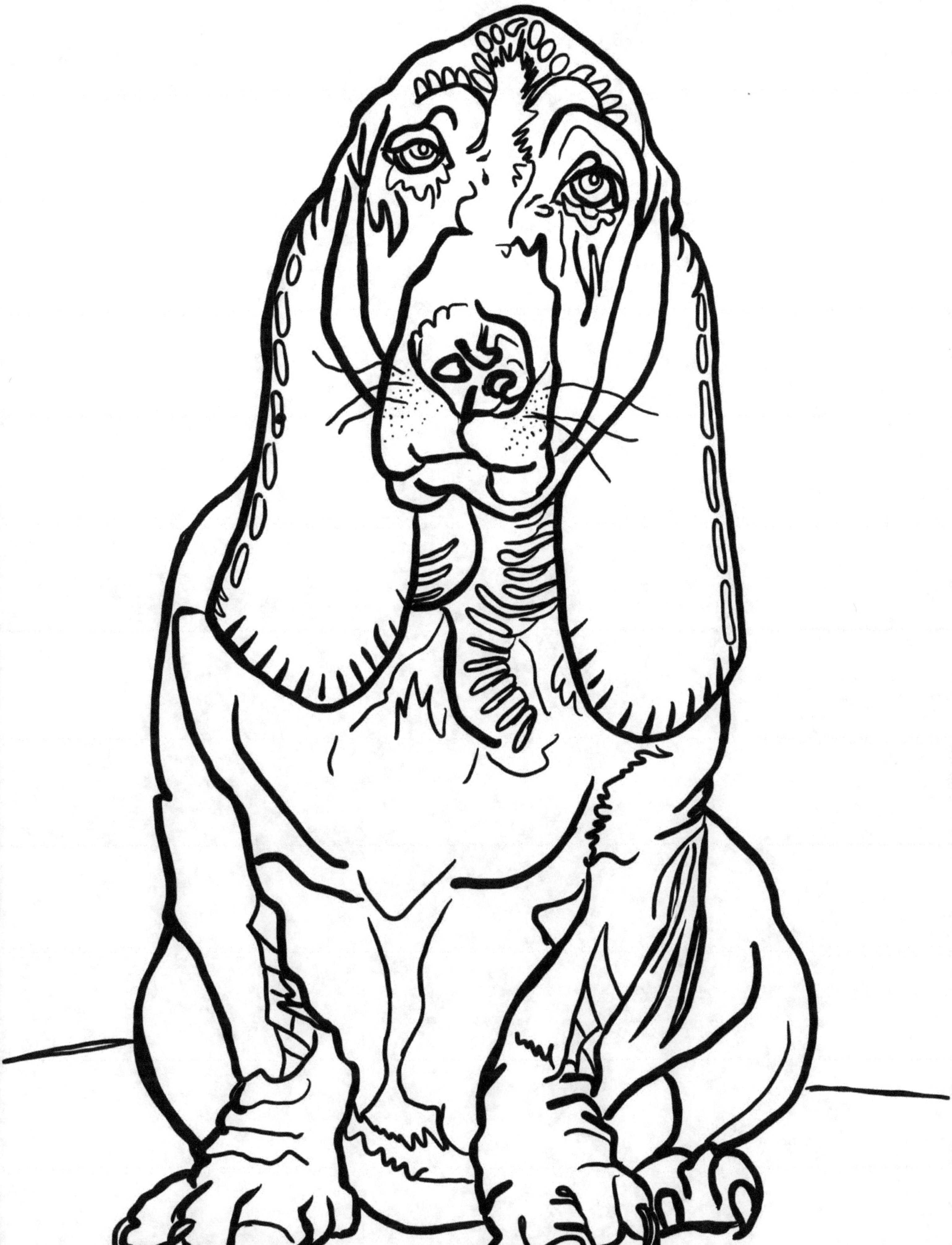

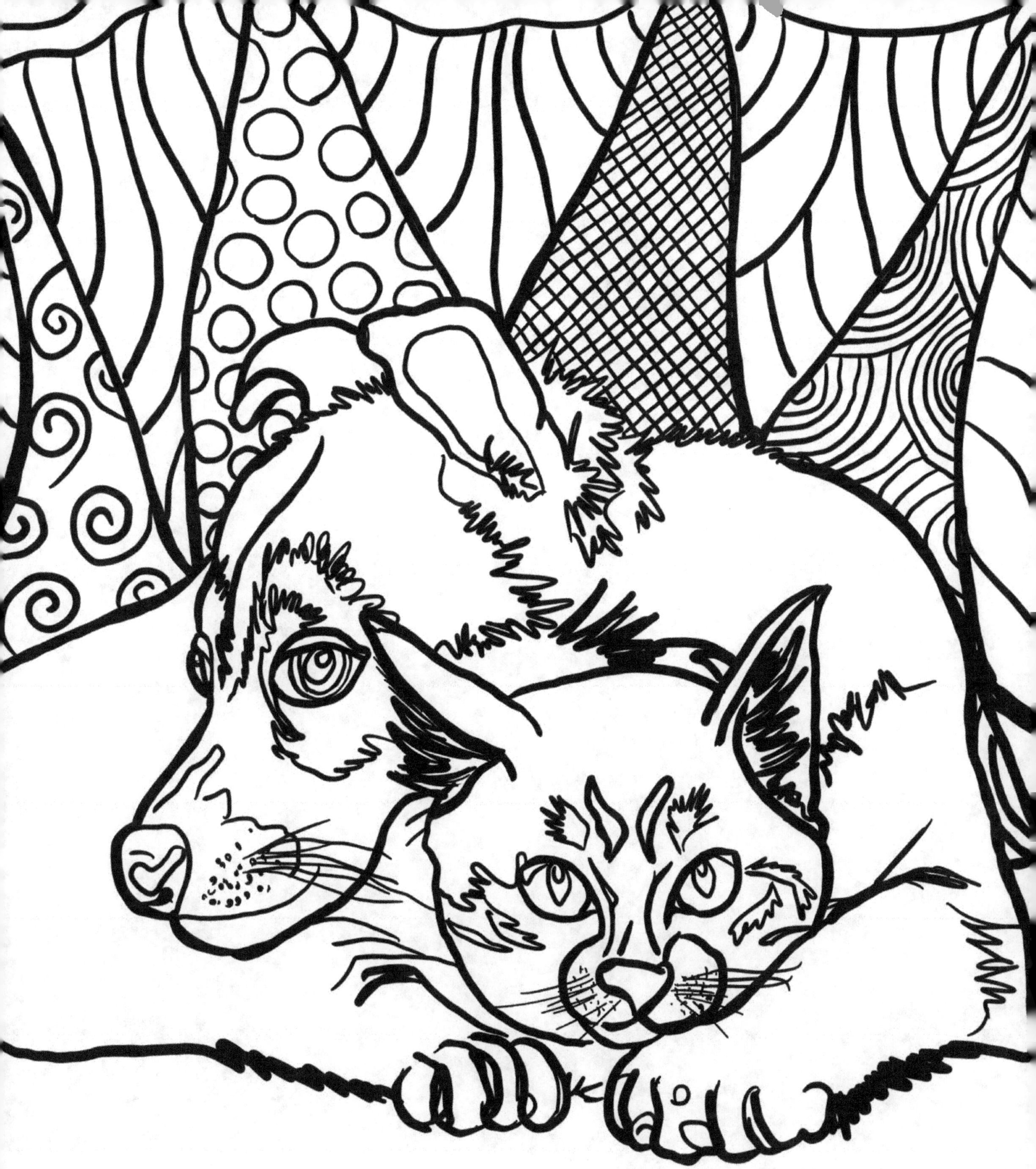

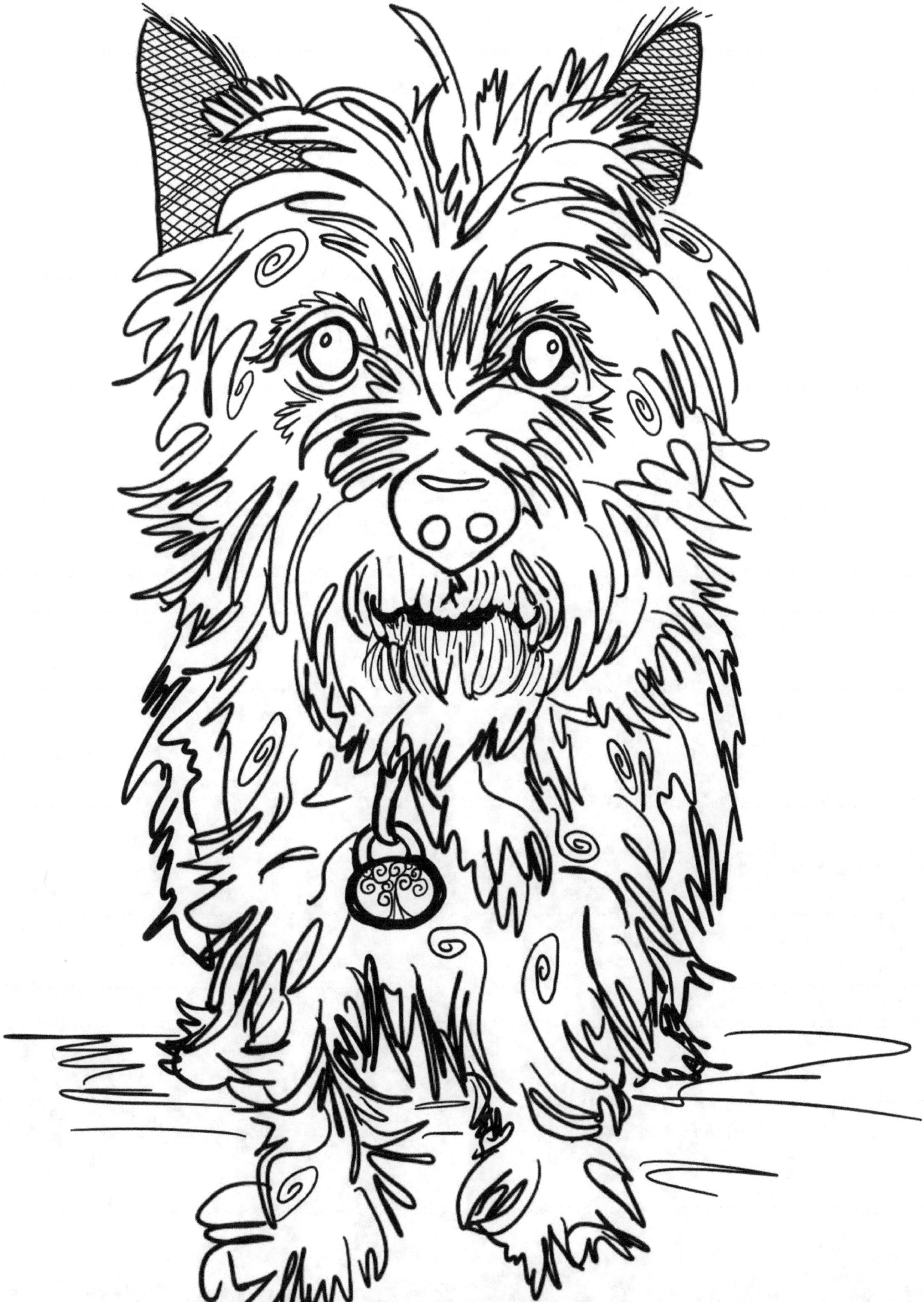

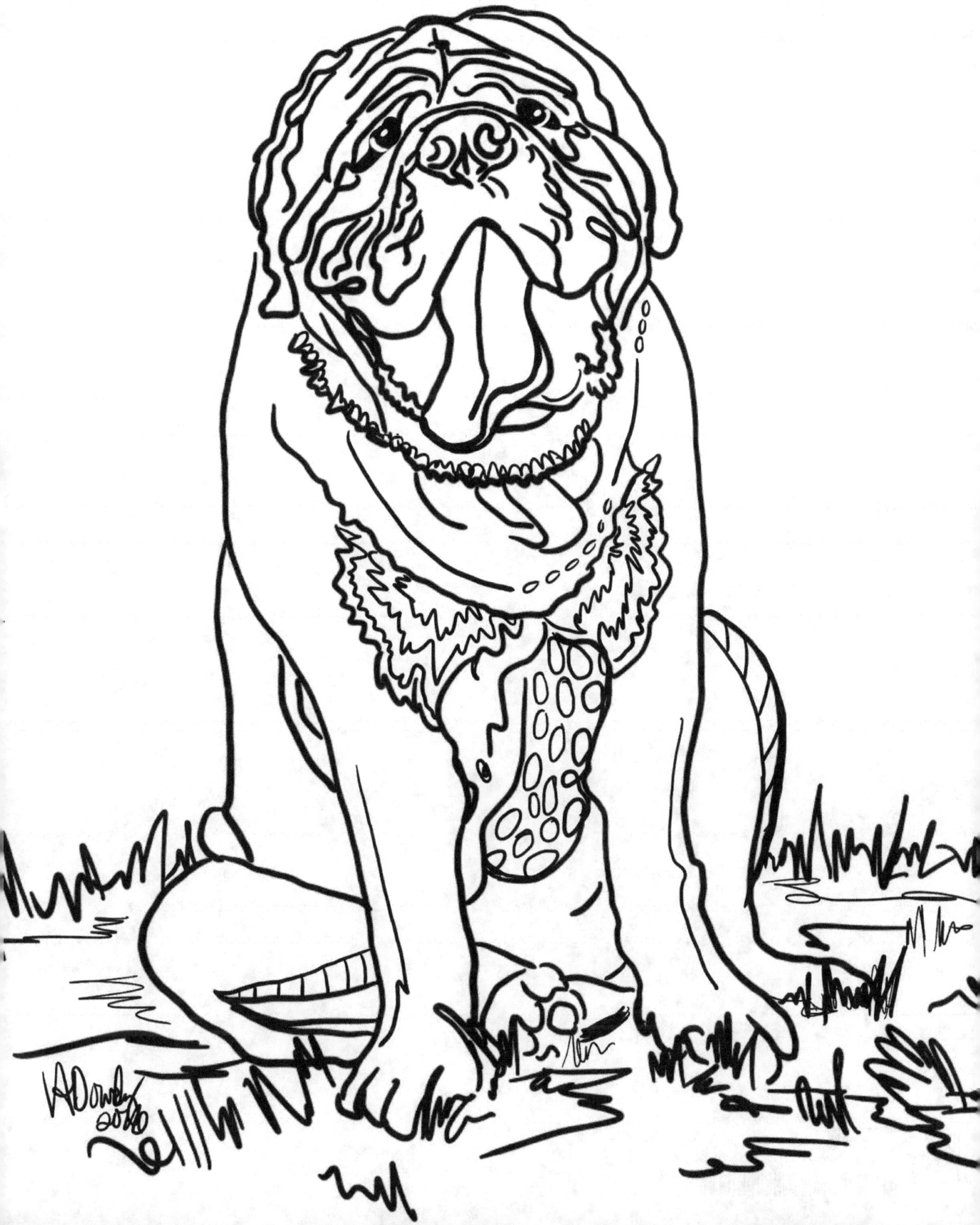

www.ingramcontent.com/pod-product-compliance
Lightning Source LLC
Chambersburg PA
CBHW081121180526
45170CB00008B/2945
9781539724469